Algebra1 Concepts
Concept-wise book series
by Vaishali Patil

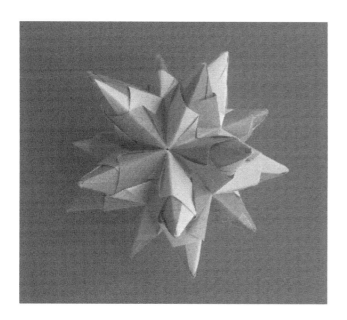

Student Name: _____

Grade: _____

School: _____

Book1: Algebra1 Concepts
Concept-wise book series by Vaishali Patil
This book includes around 250 Algebra 1 topics in an organized question and answer format. The goal is to make students understand each concept thoroughly in the correct order using examples. The topics covered are:

- **Numbers and Rules, Integers, Order of Operations**
- **Equations**
- **Systems**
- **Inequalities**
- **Exponents**
- **Quadratics**
- **Polynomials and Factoring**
- **Radicals**
- **Functions**
- **Series**
- **Graphing Linear Equations and Inequalities**
- **Quadratics and Graphing**
- **Applications**
- **Absolute Value Equations and Inequalities**

Table of Contents

Chapter1: Rules, Properties, Definitions and Order of Operations

Picture 1: Number System

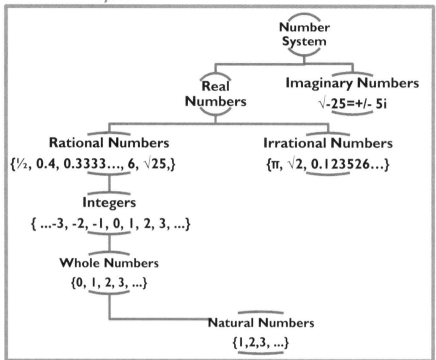

1. **What are natural numbers?**
   Natural Numbers are counting numbers starting from 1.
   {1, 2, 3, …}

2. **What are whole numbers?**
   Whole numbers are counting numbers starting from 0.
   {0, 1, 2, 3, …}

3. **What are integers?**
   Integers are negative and positive whole numbers including 0.
   {… -3, -2, -1, 0, 1, 2, 3, …}

4. **What are rational numbers?**
   Rational Numbers are numbers that can be written as a whole number, fraction or a decimal number. The decimal cannot be non-terminating or non-repeating which means it has to stop or repeat.
   {½, 0.4, 0.3333…, 6, √25, …}

5. What are irrational numbers?

Numbers that cannot be written as a fraction and/or a decimals that are non-repeating and non-terminating. These are decimals that do not repeat and do not stop. One example is π which equals 3.1415.... , its digits after the decimal don't repeat or stop. Some radicals are also irrational numbers because they cannot be expressed as a fraction. {π, √2, √35, 0.123526, ...}

6. What is the additive inverse of a number?

Additive inverse also know as opposite of a number is the same number with opposite sign. Additive inverses added together have a sum total of zero. In easy terms, change the sign of the given number to the opposite sign.
Rule: Additive inverse of a is −a
Examples: Additive inverse of 6 is −6
   Additive inverse of -1/2 is +1/2

7. What is the multiplicative inverse of a number?

Multiplicative inverse is the reciprocal of the number. Do not change the sign. Flip the number or fraction. If there is no denominator assume a denominator is one.
Rule: Multiplicative inverse of a is 1/a
Rule: Multiplicative inverse of a/b is b/a
Example: Multiplicative inverse of -3/4 is -4/3

8. What is the additive identity property?

Additive identity property states that any number added to zero is the number itself. So the additive identity is 0. Adding a zero to any number does not change that number.
Rule: a+0=a
Example: 5+0=5

9. What is the multiplicative identity property?

Multiplicative identity property states that any number multiplied by 1 is the number itself. So Multiplicative Identity is 1. Because multiplying by one does not change any number.
Rule: a x 1=a
Example: 5 x 1=5

10. What is the absolute value of a number?

Absolute value of a number is its distance from "0" on the number line. To evaluate the absolute value, in terms of signs, drop the sign from inside the absolute value symbols. Do not drop the outside sign.

Examples: |-51|=51
                -|-6|=-6
                -|4|=-4
                -|10|=-10
                |-10|=10
                -|-10|=-10

(Note: Drop sign inside the absolute value, do not drop the sign outside the absolute value)

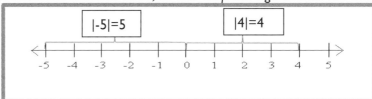

Absolute Value on a number line is the distance from 0.

11. How do you add integers?

Adding integer problems are of two kinds:

- Same sign integers addition: When adding integers of the same sign, **add their absolute** values and **keep the same sign**.

Example: (-3)+(-2)= - (3+2)= - 5

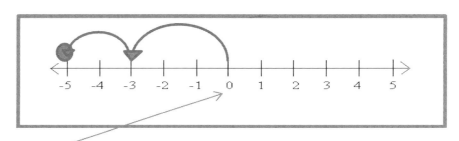

On a graph, start from zero and go to the first number, -3 here. Then jump as many places that are added. Go left for negative and right for positive. Two places left from -3 is -5.

- Adding opposite signs integers: When adding integers of the opposite signs, **subtract their absolute values** and keep the **sign of the larger absolute value number**.

Example: (-8) + (4) = -(8-4) = - 4

(Note: Same signs, Add and keep the same sign.
Opposite signs, Subtract and keep the bigger number sign.)

12. How do you subtract integers?

To subtract an integer, add its opposite. a-b = a+(-b)
Subtraction problems are solved by changing to Addition problems. Subtraction means adding the opposite. A subtraction problem is changed to an addition problem, by changing the number to the opposite sign. Follow the addition rules after that.

Example: -4 – 6 = - 4 + - 6, since they are the same sign, now add the numbers and keep the common sign negative= -10.

Example: 5-7 = 5+-7, since they are different signs, subtract and give the sign of the larger absolute value= -2.

13. How do you multiply integers?

The multiplication of integers' rules depend on the signs:
- Multiplying Same signs' integers: When multiplying integers of the same sign, multiply the absolute values and make the sign of the product **positive**.

Example: (-8)(-4) = 32
- Multiplying opposite signs' integers: When multiplying integers of the opposite sign, multiply the absolute values and make the sign of the product **negative**.

Example: (-8)(4) = -32

(Note: Same signs integer product is positive, Opposite signs integer product is negative)

14. How do you divide integers?

Two rules for dividing integers:
- Same sign integers division: When dividing integers of the same sign, divide the absolute values and make the sign of the quotient **positive**.

Example: (-8)/(-4) = 2
- Dividing opposite signs integers: When dividing integers of the opposite signs, divide the absolute values and make the sign of the quotient **negative**.

Example: (-8)/(4) = -2

(Note: Same signs quotient is positive, opposite signs quotient is negative)

15. What is the order of operations?

Given a set of numbers and operations with grouping symbols, use the following order when simplifying expressions of numbers:

Parenthesis/Groups
Exponents
Multiply or Divide (equal priority, simplify left to right)
Add or Subtract (equal priority, simplify left to right)

(Note: Hint to remember: Please Excuse My Dear Aunt Sally)

Example:

$2[(12 \bullet 2)\, 3 - 16] + (11 - 6)$	(Inside parenthesis first)
$2[(24)\, 3 - 16] + 5$	(Left to right multiply, since it came first)
$=2[72- 16] + 5$	(Subtract inside parenthesis)
$=2[56] + 5$	(Multiply)
$=112+5$	(Add/Subtract last)
$=117$	(Final Answer)

Example:

$2-\frac{5}{4}(8\text{-}3)^2+\frac{3}{4}-3^2$	(Inside parenthesis first)
$=2-\frac{5}{4}(5)^2+\frac{3}{4}-3^2$	(Exponents)
$=2-\frac{5}{4}(25)+\frac{3}{4}-9$	(Multiply)
$=2-\frac{125}{4}+\frac{3}{4}-9$	(Add/subtract left to right)
$=2-\frac{122}{4}-9$	(Add/subtract left to right)
$=\frac{8}{4}-\frac{122}{4}-\frac{36}{4}$	(Subtract)
$=-37\frac{1}{2}$	(Final Answer)

(Note another tip here: An easy way to remember this is do all the additions and subtractions outside of parenthesis last)

16. **Amongst the two, do you multiply first or add first in simplifying numerical expressions using order of operations?**
Multiplication and division takes precedence over addition and subtraction.
Example: $2+3(5)$
Solution: Here we multiply first $3.5 = 15$ even though add appears first.
Then add, $2+15=17$

17. **Amongst the two, do you multiply first or divide first in simplifying numerical expressions using order of operations?**
Multiplication and division have the same order of preference. The order depends on which comes first when simplifying from left to right.
Example: $\frac{15}{5}+5.4$
Solution:

$\frac{15}{5}=3$	(Divide first since it came before multiply)
$5.4 = 20$	(Then multiply)
$3+20=23$	(Finally add)

18. **Amongst the two, do you add or subtract first in simplifying numerical expressions using order of operations?**
   Both addition and subtraction have equal preference. The order depends on which comes first when simplifying from left to right.

19. **Which operations take precedence after groups and exponents?**
   Multiplication, division take precedence over addition, subtraction.

20. **What is a variable?**
   A variable usually represented by an alphabet, is the unknown quantity we are solving for in the problem.
   Example: $3x + 5 = 8$, here "x" is the variable

21. **What is a coefficient?**
   The number multiplied in front of the variable is called the coefficient, if there isn't any number, the coefficient is a 1.
   Example: $5x^3$, Coefficient is 5
                     x^5, Coefficient is 1

22. **What is a constant term?**
   A constant term is just a number, without a variable attached to it.
   Example: $5x + 10$, Constant is 10

Expression

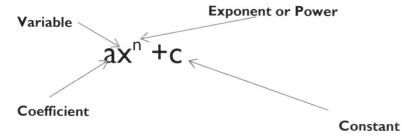

23. **What is a monomial?**
   Monomial means a single term. It can be a product(combination) of coefficients and variables to different degrees, all the numbers and variables are multiplied together (there are no "+" or "-" signs separating the coefficents of variables) and is of the form (Coefficient)$x^n y^m$...
   Examples: $20x^2y^2$(Monomial) 10(Monomial and just a constant)
                     $3x$(Monomial) $5y$(Monomial)

24. What is a polynomial?

A polynomial is a combination of one or more terms of monomials and constants combined through addition and subtraction.

Example: $3x^2-4y+6z$ (polynomial)

25. What is the degree of a polynomial?

The degree of a polynomial is the highest power of any term in the polynomial. If a term has more than one variable, add the exponents of different variables to get the power of the polynomial. Do not add powers of separate terms together.

Example: What is the degree of the polynomial $4x^3 y^7 - x^7 y^7 + 5x^3 y^5$

Solution: First term has $3+7 = 10$ variables.

Second term has $7+7 = 14$ variables.

Third term has $3+5 = 8$ variables.

The degree of the given polynomial is 14 since that's the highest power term.

26. If there is no coefficient in front of a variable what do you assume it to be?

If there is no coefficient in front of a variable you assume it to be 1.

Example: $3x^2+5y+z$. Here, the coefficient of z is 1.

27. If there is no coefficient in front of a negative variable, what do you assume it to be?

If there is no coefficient in front of a variable you assume it to be -1.

Example: $3x-y$, Here the coefficient of y is -1.

28. What is an expression?

A combination of monomials formed by addition or subtraction is an expression.

Example: $3x-4y^2$, this is an expression.

29. What is the naming convention for polynomials based on the number of terms?

The naming convention for polynomials based on the number of terms is as follows:

One term– Monomial

Example: x^2y^2

Two terms– Binomial

Example: y^2+x^3

Three terms– Trinomial

Example: y^2+x^3+5x

Four terms or more– Polynomial

Example: $x^2y^2+x^3+3y^2+8$

30. **What is the naming convention for polynomials based on the degree of polynomials?**

The naming convention for polynomials based on the degree of the polynomial is as follows:

Degree One– Linear

Example: $x+2y+4$

Degree Two– Quadratic

Example: $y+x^2+4x+4$

Degree Three– Cubic

Example: y^2+x^3+5x

Degree Four– Quartic

Example: $x^4+x^3+3y^2+8$

Degree Five– Quintic

Example: $x^2y^3+x^2y^2z+z^4+10x$

Chapter2: Equations

- What are we going to learn about Equations?
  - Solving equations in one variable
  - Addition Property of Equality
  - Multiplication Property of Equality
  - Opposite Operations
  - Distributive Property
  - Transposing terms
  - Solving Equations with one or more fractions
  - Solving System of Equations by Graphing Method
  - Solving System of Equations by Substitution Method
  - Solving System of Equations by Addition Method
  - Consistent and Inconsistent Systems
  - Dependent and Independent Systems

31. What is an equation?

An equation is a relationship between variables and numbers. An equation is represented by two expressions combined with an equal sign.
Example: $3x+6y= 4x-5y$

32. What is the Addition Property of Equality?

If $a = b$, then $a \underline{+ c} = b \underline{+ c}$
Adding a new term "c" on both sides will not change the value of the original equation. This is the Addition Property of Equality. This is useful in solving equations
Example: Given an equation, $x-5=6$
   Then $x-5+5=6+5$. Here we added 5 on both sides. This does not change the original equality.

33. What is the Multiplication Property of Equality?

If $a = b$, then $a.c = b.c$
Multiplying by a new term on both sides will not change the value of the original equation. This is the Multiplication Property of Equality.
Example: Given $\frac{1}{2} x =6$
   Then $2(\frac{1}{2} x)=2(6)$ here we multiplied by 2 on both sides. This does not change the equality and simplifies solving for x.

34. What is the Distributive Property?

$a(b+c) = a.b + a.c$
Given a number attached to outside of the parenthesis of an expression, it multiplies to every single term along with its sign, separated by plus or minus, inside the parenthesis.

(Note: There is no sign between the outside number and the parenthesis. If there was a sign between "a" and the parenthesis you cannot distribute. It would be add or subtraction operation.)

Example: $\frac{3}{4}$(x+3)-2(x-5) (Multiply the outside number with its sign to each of the inside numbers with their signs. In the first group the outside number (3/4) is multiplied to (x) and (+3); In the second group the outside number(-2) is multiplied to (x) and (-5))

Solution: $=(\frac{3}{4})(x)+(\frac{3}{4})(3)+(-2)(x) -2(-5)$

$= \frac{3}{4}x + \frac{9}{4} -2x+10 = -\frac{5}{4}x+\frac{49}{4} = -\frac{5}{4}x+12\frac{1}{4}$

Here we multiply the outside number to each of the terms inside the parenthesis. This is called distribution. Be sure to multiply the signs of both outside and inside numbers.

---

35. **How do you multiply whole numbers with fractions when distributing?**

You only multiply numerator with numerator and denominator with denominator. If there is no denominator place a placeholder 1 there.

Example: $-\frac{2}{3}$(2x-6)

Solution:

$(-\frac{2}{3}).(\frac{2}{1}x) +(-\frac{2}{3}).(-\frac{6}{1})$	(Distribute and multiply)
$-\frac{4x}{3} + 4$	(Final Answer)

---

36. **What does solving an equation mean?**

Solving an equation means to find the values or variables that make the equation true. This is accomplished by isolating the unknown variable to one side of the equation.
Example: Solve the equation 4x=48.
Solution: Dividing by 4 on both sides we get x=12. To check, plug in 12 for x and see if that makes it a true statement. 4(12)=48. True. So 12 is a solution to 4x=48.

---

37. **What does transposing terms to the other side of an equation mean?**

Transposing terms means to take the term to the other side. Transposing an addition term becomes subtraction on the other side of the equation and subtraction becomes addition just like opposite operations. Multiplication becomes division and division becomes multiplication when transposed to the other side of an equation.

Example: Transpose 4 in 4x=48. Since 4 is multiplied on the left side it divides on the right side. x=48/4.
Transpose "3x" to the right side 5-3x=7x+10. Since "3x" is subtracted on the left side it is added on the right side. 5=7x+10+3x.

38. **What questions do you ask yourself when trying to solve an equation for a variable?**

    Can I add or subtract a number on both sides?
    Can I multiply or divide on both sides?
    What can I do on both sides of the equation to isolate the variable?
    What opposite operation can I apply to both sides?
    Can I transpose some terms to the other side?

39. **How do you solve an equation in one variable?**

    A. Equations can be solved with the transpose method. Transpose means to move terms to the other side of the equation. Transposing an added/subtracted term becomes opposite and vice versa. A multiplied/divided term becomes its reciprocal on the other side.

    Example: $3x - 1/5 = 7/5$

    Solution: Our goal is to isolate the variable we are trying to solve for.
    So we transpose $-1/5$ to the other side of the equation. Then $-1/5$ becomes $+1/5$.
    And the equation becomes, $3x = 7/5 + 1/5$
    Adding like terms, $3x = 8/5$
    Now we transpose the coefficient 3 to the right side. The 3 becomes $(1/3)$
    Applying the multiply/divide opposite operation on both sides.
    $x = (1/3)(8/5)$
    Final answer by simplifying gives $x = 8/15$

    B. Equations are also solved by **opposite operations method with the goal to** isolate the required variable. Remember, opposite operation of add is subtract. Opposite operation of multiply is divide, opposite operation of subtract is add, opposite operation of divide is multiply. If there are no parenthesis, add/subtract opposite operations are done first then multiply/divide. With fractions, if "x" is multiplied by a fraction, the opposite operation would be to multiply by the reciprocal of the fraction. Equations can also be solved by transposing terms to other side to isolate the required variable.

    Example: $3x - 1/5 = 7/5$

    Solution: What is the opposite operation of $-1/5$? Opposite operation of $-1/5$ is $+1/5$.
    Apply the add/subtract opposite operation on both sides, $3x - 1/5 + 1/5 = 7/5 + 1/5$
    $3x = 8/5$
    Applying the multiply/divide opposite operation on both sides.
    $3x/3 = (1/3)(8/5)$
    $x = 8/15$

Example: $\frac{3}{4}x + 5 = -\frac{5}{2}$
Solution:

$\frac{3}{4}x + 5 - 5 = -\frac{5}{2} - 5$	(Subtract 5 on both sides)
$\frac{3}{4}x = -\frac{15}{2}$	(Simplify)
$(\frac{4}{3})(\frac{3}{4}x) = \frac{4}{3} \cdot (-\frac{15}{2})$	(Multiply both sides by the reciprocal of $\frac{3}{4}$ which is $\frac{4}{3}$)
$x = -\frac{60}{6} = -10$	(Final Answer)

40. **How do you solve an equation with variables on both sides?**

To solve equations with variables on both sides, bring the variable to one side and constants to the other side. Equations are solved by **opposite operations** to **isolate** the required variable.

Example: $\frac{3}{4}x - 5 = \frac{1}{2}(x+14)$
Solution:

$\frac{3}{4}x - 5 = \frac{1}{2}x + 7$	(Distribute ½ on the right side)
$4(\frac{3}{4}x - 5 = \frac{1}{2}x + 7)$	(Mulitply by LCM on both sides, LCM of 4, 2 = 4)
$3x - 20 = 2x + 28$	(Simplify)
$3x - 2x = 28 + 20$	(Subtract 2x on both sides, Add 20 to both sides)
$x = 48$	(Combining the like terms together)

41. **How do you solve an equation in two variables?**

Given an equation in "x" and "y" and solving for "y". If solving for "y", bring all the "y" terms to one side, combine them into one term of "y" and then isolate the variable "y". Take all the other variables and constant terms to the other side.

Example - $\frac{3}{4}(x-2) + \frac{4}{5}y = 8$. Solve for "y".
Solution:

$\frac{4}{5}y = \frac{3}{4}(x-2) + 8$	(Take the "x" terms to the right side)
$\frac{4}{5}y = \frac{3}{4}(x) - \frac{3}{4}(2) + 8$	(Distribute 3/4)
$\frac{4}{5}y = \frac{3}{4}(x) - \frac{3}{2} + 8$	(Simplify)
$(\frac{5}{4})\frac{4}{5}y = (\frac{5}{4})\frac{3}{4}(x) - (\frac{5}{4})\frac{3}{2} + (\frac{5}{4})8$	(Mulitply by reciprocal of "y's coefficient to isolate "y")
$y = \frac{15}{16}(x) - \frac{15}{8} + \frac{40}{4}$	(Multiply each term by 5/4)
$y = \frac{15}{16}(x) + 8\frac{1}{8}$	(Combine like terms, final answer)

42. How do you solve an equation with fractions?

To solve an equation with fractions, try to get rid of the fractions by multiplying each term on both sides by least common denominator(LCM) of all the denominators. Then solve using opposite operations.

Example: $\frac{2}{3}(x+5) = \frac{1}{4} + 2x$

Solution: LCM of 3 and 4 is 12. So multiply each term by 12 or 12/1

$$(\tfrac{12}{1}).\tfrac{2}{3}(x+5) = \left(\tfrac{12}{1}\right).\tfrac{1}{4} + (\tfrac{12}{1}).2x$$

(Note: When multiplying by 12 on the left side only multiply the outside fraction by it because it's a group. On the right side, the terms are separate so each term gets multiplied by 12.)
Simplifying,

$(\tfrac{12}{1}).\tfrac{2}{3}(x+5) = \left(\tfrac{12}{1}\right).\tfrac{1}{4} + (\tfrac{12}{1}).2x$	(Multiply each term by 12 or 12/1)
$8(x+5)=3+24x$	(Simplify coefficients)
$8x+40=3+24x$	(Distribute the 8 to "x" and 5)
$40-3=24x-8x$	(Isolate "x" to one side)
$37=16x$	(Divide by 16)
$x=\frac{37}{16} = 2\frac{5}{16}$	(Final Answer)

43. How do you solve an equation with one fraction on each side?

To solve equations with one fraction on each side, cross multiply and solve like proportions.

Example: $\frac{x+5}{3} = \frac{1}{4}$

Solution:

$\frac{x+5}{3} = \frac{1}{4}$	(Given)
$4(x+5) = 1(3)$	(Cross multiply using parenthesis)
$4x+20=3$	(Distribute 4)
$4x = 3-20$	(Isolate x to one side)
$4x = -17$	(Divide by 4 on both sides)
$x = -\frac{17}{4} = -4\,¼$	(Final Answer)

44. How do you solve an equation with decimals?

To solve an equation with decimals, you can either work with decimals and solve using opposite operations or convert all of the decimals to integer numbers by multiplying each term by highest power of 10 needed and solve by opposite operations method.
(Note: You have to multiply by the same power of 10 throughout you cannot just move the decimals unevenly.)
Example: $0.35x + 20 = 0.5x + 11$
Solution: This equation has numbers in its hundredth place so multiply the entire equation by 100.

A. First Method

$100(0.35x) + 100(20) = 100(0.5x) + 100(11)$ $35x + 2000 = 50x + 1100$ $35x - 50x = 1100 - 2000$ $-15x = -900$ $x = 60$	(Muliply each term by 100) (Isolate "x" using Opposite operations) (Divide by -15 on both sides) (Final Answer)

B. Another method is to continue working with decimals

$0.35x + 20 = 0.5x + 11$ $0.35x - .50x = 11 - 20$ $.15x = -9$ $-.15x = -9$ $x = 60$	(Isolate "x" using Opposite operations) (Subtract) (Divide by -.15 on both sides) (Final Answer)

45. **When do you plot solutions on the number line and when do you plot them on the coordinate axis?**

One variable equations' solutions are plotted on a number line and two variable solutions on the coordinate axes.

Examples:

Numberline graphs: $x > 2$ (one variable x)

Coordinate axes: $y = 4x + 3$ (Two variables x, y)

Chapter 3: Inequalities

- What are we going to learn about Inequalities?
  - Solving inequalities in one variable
  - Negative Multilpication or Division <u>Reverse Inequality Rule</u> in solving inequalities
  - Graphing one variable inequality on a number line
  - Interval notation

46. **How do you solve an inequality in one variable?**

Inequalities like equations are solved by transposing terms or by **opposite operations** to isolate the required variable.

(Note: The only difference between solving equations and solving inequalities is that the inequality reverses if you <u>multiply</u> or <u>divide</u> by a negative number on both sides.)

If multiplied or divided by a negative number inequality reverses

<u>Reversed</u>

$\geq$	becomes	$\leq$
$\leq$	becomes	$\geq$
$>$	becomes	$<$
$<$	becomes	$>$

Example: Solve -3x-5 > 7

Solution:

-3x>7+5	(Transpose -5 to right side /Opposite operation of -5 is +5 on both sides)
-3x>12	(Inequality does not reverse for add subtract operations)
-3x/-3<12/-3	(Division by -3 on both sides and reverse inequality due to division by negative number)
x<-4	(Final Answer)

47. **What is the most important rule in solving linear Inequalities?**

The inequality reverses if you multiply or divide by a negative number on both sides.

Example: Solve $\frac{-3}{5}x > 21$

Solution:

$\frac{-5}{3} \cdot \frac{-3}{5}x < \frac{-5}{3} \cdot 21$	(Multiply both sides by -5/3)
	(The inequality sign reverses due to multiplying by a negative number)
$\frac{-5}{3} \cdot \frac{-3}{5}x < \frac{-5}{3} \cdot \frac{21}{1}$	(This cancels the fractions on the left side x< -105/3)

x< -35   (Final Answer)

48. How do you graph an inequality in one variable on a number line?

- **Greater than:** To the right with the point not included

Example: Graph x>4 on the number line(Not including 4 represented as a open circle)

Picture5: Greater than and one variable only inequalities graph

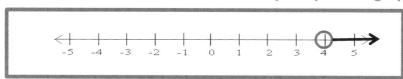

Interval: (4, ∞)

- **Greater than or equal to:** To the right with the point included

Example: Graph x≥4 on the number line(Including 4 represented as a closed circle right)

Picture7: Greater than or equal to one variable inequality graph

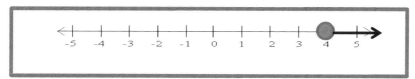

Interval: [4, ∞)

- **Less than:** To the left on the number line

Example: Graph x<4 on the number line(Not including 4 represented as a open circle left)

Picture6: Less than one variable inequality graph

Interval: (-∞, 4)

- **Less than or equal to:** To the left with the point included

Example: Graph x≤4 on the number line(Including 4 represented as a closed circle left)

Picture8: Less than or equal to one variable inequality graph

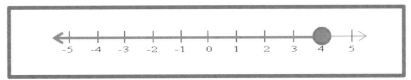

Interval: (-∞, 4]

---

49. **What is the interval notation of writing the solution?**
Interval Notation means writing the answer as it lies on the number line range using endpoints.
Example: If "x" lies between -4 and 5, and endpoints are not included then x=(-4,5)

---

50. **What is the convention for using brackets or parenthesis in interval notation?**
Using brackets vs parenthesis depend on whether the points are <u>included</u> or <u>excluded</u>.
- If the inequality <u>does not include</u> the endpoint number in the solution, use <u>parenthesis.</u> For less than and greater than inequalities. <, >
- If the inequality includes the number, as in less than or equal to or greater than or equal to use <u>brackets</u>. ≤, ≥
- Infinity is used when the inequality is one sided. Infinity always gets parenthesis not brackets since it's not a particular number.
- If there is more than one interval, they are written together with a union sign "U".

Example: x<-4	Written as (-∞, -4) in interval notation. (Endpoint not included:parenthesis)
Example: x≤-4	Written as (-∞, -4] in interval notation. (Endpoint included:bracket)
Example: x>-4	Written as (-4, ∞) in interval notation.
Example: x≥4	Written as [4, ∞) in interval notation.
Example: -4< x <5	Written as (-4,5)
Example: -4≤ x ≤5	Written as [-4,5]
Example: x<4 and x≥5	Written as (-∞, -4)U[5, ∞)

Chapter 4: Functions

- What are we going to learn about functions?
  - Definition of a function
  - Domain and Range
  - Vertical line test
  - Discrete functions
  - Continuous functions
  - Direct Variation
  - Inverse Variation
  - Proportionality Constant

51. What are independent and dependent variables?

An independent variable is the input or cause and dependent variable is the output or effect.

Example: The students test score depends on the number of hours he practices math.

52. How do you define a function?

A function is a relation or a mapping between two variables in which for each "x" value (independent variable), there is only one corresponding value of "y"(dependent variable).   This means "x" cannot repeat.

Example: Function: {(1,2)(2,4)(4,5)}

Not a function: {(1,2)(1,3)(4,5)(7,8)} (For x=1, there are two different values for y)

Picture9: Function Mapping One-to-One

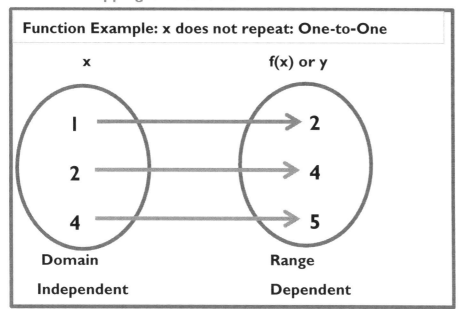

Function Example: x does not repeat: One-to-One

x   f(x) or y

1 → 2
2 → 4
4 → 5

Domain   **Range**

Independent   **Dependent**

Picture10: Not a function mapping One-to-Many

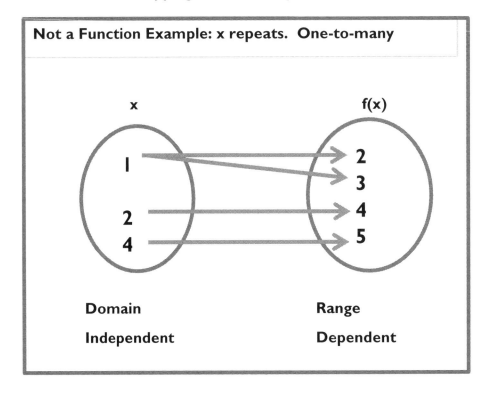

Picture11: Function Mapping Many-to-One

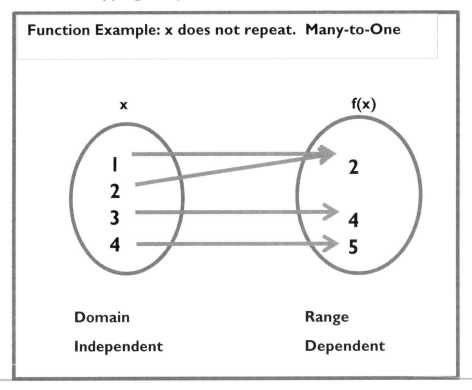

53. What does it mean to <u>evaluate</u> a function?

To <u>evaluate</u> means to find the "value" of the function by substituting or plugging in "values" for the variable of the function and simplifying.

Example: $f(x)=-3x^2+6x+4$, Evaluate $f(-3)$

Solution:

$f(x)=-3x^2+6x+4$

$f(-3) =-3(-3)^2+6(-3)+4$	(Replace all x's with -3)
$=-3(9)+6(-3)+4$	(Simplify)
$= -27-18+4$	
$= -41$	(Final Answer)

Example: $f(x) = -3(x)^2+6x+4$, Evaluate $f(2b)$

Solution: $f(x) = -3(x)^2+6x+4$

$f(2b) = -3(2b)^2+6(2b)+4$	(Replace x with 2b)
$=-3(4b^2)+6(2b)+4$	(Simplify)
$=-12b^2+12b+4$	(Final Answer)

54. If f(x) is given, how do you find x?

f(x) or y is the range of the function.

Example: $f(x) = 5x^2+10$, if $f(x)=135$ find x

Solution: Substitute given value for "y" or f(x) (Do not plug in for "x" value)

$f(x) = 5x^2+10$	
$135 = 5x^2+10$	(Replace f(x) with 135 and solve for x)
$135-10=5x^2$	(Subtract 10 on both sides)
$125=5x^2$	
$125/5 =x^2$	(Divide by 5 on both sides)
$25=x^2$	(Take the square root on both sides)
$\pm5=x$	(Final Answer)

55. What is the domain of a function?

The input or independent values the function can take is called the domain. The x-values are the independent values. For discrete functions, the domain is separate points. For continuous functions, it is an interval of x-values from lowest to highest (left to right on the x axis)

Example: Find the domain from the ordered pairs or discrete function:

{(1,3)(-1,4)(5, 7)(3,10)}

Solution: x value are the domain values: {-1,1,3,5}

Example: Find the domain from the graph of a function. Domain is the interval of "x-values" from left to right.

Picture12: Domain from a graph

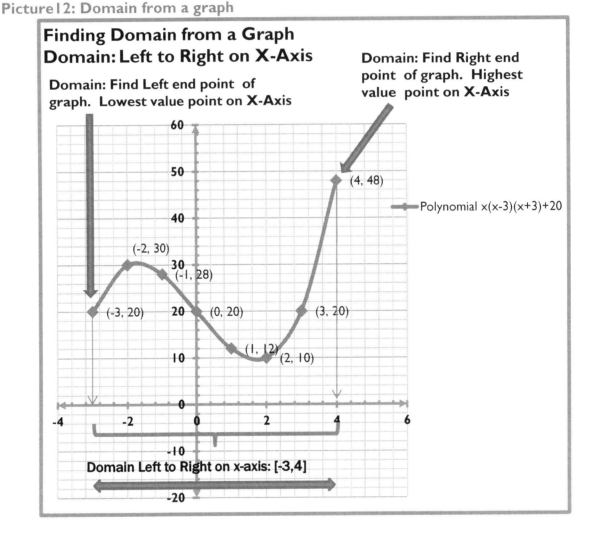

56. What is the range of a function?

Range of a function is the output or the dependent values the function can take.
The y–values are the dependent values. For discrete functions, the range is separate points. For continuous functions the range is an interval of y-values from lowest to highest or lowest to highest on the y-axis.

Example: Find the range from the ordered pairs {(1,3)(-1,4)(5, 7)(3,10)}
Solution: y-values are the range values: {3,4,7,10}

Picture13: Range from a graph

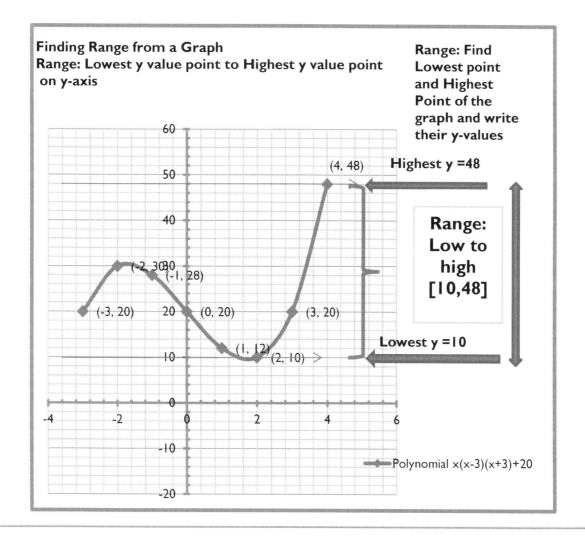

57. What is a discrete function?

A function with separate points or discrete points that are not connected by a line. This implies that the points in between the given points are not included.

Example: f(x)={(-4,-2),(-1,4), (0,3),(2,4),(3.5,3.7),(4,9),(5,8)}

Picture14: Discrete Function Graph

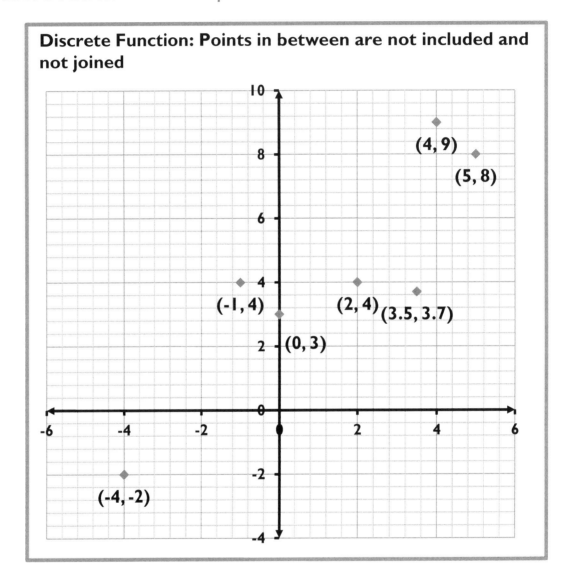

© Vaishali Patil

58. What is a continuous function?

A function is continuous when the points included on the graph are connected by a line.

Example: $y = 0.0508x^3 - 0.0897x^2 + 0.2131x + 3.6352$

Picture15: Continuous Function

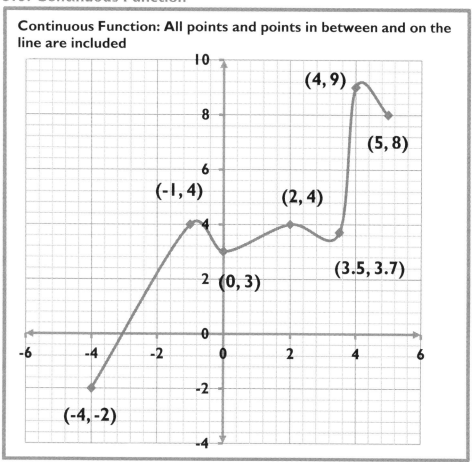

59. What does the equation of a continuous function look like?

A continuous function could be any polynomial function. It may or may not have one single equation defining it.

Example: $f(x) = x^3 + 2x + 4$

60. What does the equation of a discrete function look like?

A discrete function does not have a particular equation. It is generally given as ordered pairs.

Example: $f(x) = \{(1,3), (4, 6), (5,7)\}$

61. What is the vertical line test for a function?

To test if a graph/relation is a function, draw several vertical lines through the graph at different points and each line should not cross the graph more than once at any point. Vertical lines are not functions.

Picture16: Vertical line test for Functions

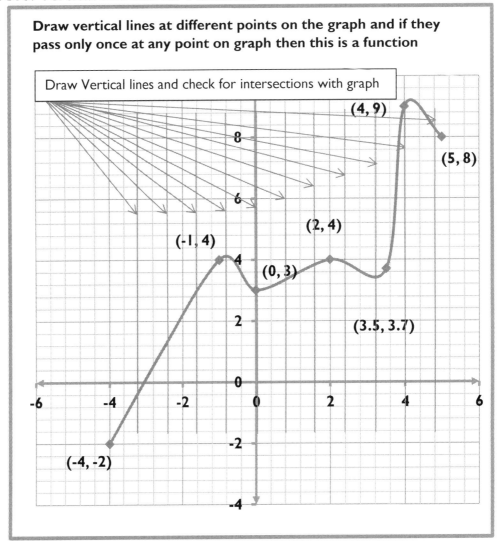

Draw vertical lines at different points on the graph and if they pass only once at any point on graph then this is a function

Draw Vertical lines and check for intersections with graph

(Each vertical line passes only once at any point on graph so this is a function.)

62. What is the other test that can be used to find whether a relation is a function or not?

If given a set of ordered pairs, check to see if "x" repeats or not. If the "x" value repeats it is not a function.

63. How do you draw a graph with a restricted domain?

When a graph is given a restricted domain, the x-values of the graph can only lie between those two points(the endpoints are included if inequality also has equal signs). The graph does not extend beyond those points.

Picture17: Restricted Domain Function graph

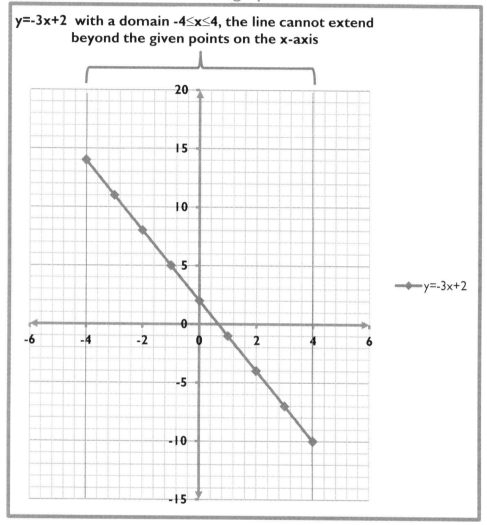

64. What is a direct variation?

In a direct variation, when "x" increases, "y" increases and when "x" decreases, "y" decreases proportionally. When the dependent variable of a function is directly proportional to the independent variable meaning it is the product of a constant and the independent value then it is a direct variation relationship. $y = kx$

Example: The pressure of a gas in a container is directly proportional to the temperature. If the pressure is 20kPA when the temperature is 10K then find the equation.

Solution: P=kT.   First find the constant of proportionality using given information by substitution and solving 20=k(10) (Here "P" is the

pressure and "T" is the temperature)

20= k.10

20/10= k

(Note: In direct variation divide y/x to find "k")

k = 20/10 =2. Now substitute k into the original equation.

Equation: P= 2 T

---

65. Does a direct variation graph pass through the origin?

Yes, the direct variation graph passes through the origin because it's a linear graph without a y-intercept. **Example:** y=2.5x

Picture18: Direct Variation Graph

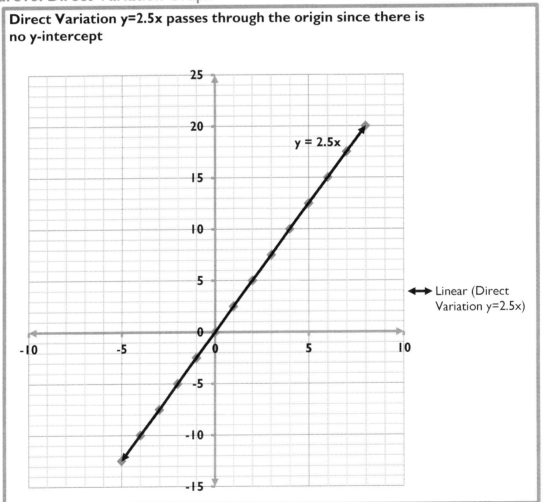

Direct Variation y=2.5x passes through the origin since there is no y-intercept

---

66. What is a direct variation proportion?

Direct variation proportion $\boxed{y_1/x_1 = y_2/x_2}$

Example: Pressure "P" is directly proportional to the temperature "T". If P=20kPA at T=10K then find P at T=25K

Solution: Using the direct variation proportion,

$P_1/T_1 = P_2/T_2$

$20/10 = P_2/25$

$(20\times25)/10 = P_2$; $P_2 = 50$kPA

67. How do you find the proportionality constant for a direct variation?

Direct Variation constant of proportionality "k" is found by dividing the dependent variable by the independent variable, formula $\boxed{k = y/x}$

Example: The height "h" of a projectile varies directly as its time "t". It takes 20 seconds to reach a height of 200 feet. Find the constant of variation.

Solution: Since it is a direct variation, $h=kt^2$

$200=k(20)^2$

$200/400 = k$

$k = \frac{1}{2}$

68. What is an inverse variation?

In an inverse variation, when "x" increases, "y" decreases and when "x" decreases, "y" increases proportionally.   When the dependent variable of a function is inversely proportional to the independent variable(it is the quotient of a constant and the independent value) then it is an inverse variation relationship.

$\boxed{y = k/x}$

Example: When one variable increases and another variable decreases proportionally then it is an inverse variation. The pressure of a gas "P" varies inversely as its volume "V" when temperature is held constant.   If Pressure is 20kPA for volume 2 cu ft. then find the volume when the pressure is 60 kPA.

Solution: Since this is an inverse proportionality,

$P=k/V$

$20 = k/2$ (Plug in given values)

$k=40$

Use the above value of "k" in the equation to find the missing variable for the second part. $P=40/V$

$60=40/V$

$V=40/60 = 2/3$ cu ft.

69. What is the inverse variation proportion?

Inverse variation proportion: $x_1y_1=x_2y_2$

Example: Mass and velocity are inversely proportional to each other. If the mass is 10 kg velocity is 30 m/s. If mass is 15 kg find the velocity.

Solution: Using the inverse variation proportion,

$x_1y_1=x_2y_2$

$m_1v_1=m_2v_2$ (Note that we can represent variables with any letters. Here "m" and "v" are more intuitive to represent mass(m) and velocity(v))

Here $m_1=10$, $v_1=30$, $m_2=15$, $v_2=?$

$10(30)=15(v_2)$

$v_2=300/15 = 20$ m/s

70. How do you find the proportionality constant for an inverse variation?

Inverse Variation constant of proportionality is found by multiplying the x and y values

$k=xy$

Example: Find the constant of variation where "y" varies inversely as "x" for the values given that y = 4 when x = 8.

Solution: Multiply the "x" and "y" values to find "k" for inverse variation.

$k=4(8)=32$

Summary of Direct and Inverse Variation

	Direct Variation	Inverse Variation
x Increases	y Increases	y Decreases
x Decreases	y Decreases	y Increases
Equation	y=kx	y=k/x
Constant of Proportionality	k=y/x	k=y.x
Proportion	$y_1/x_1=y_2/x_2$	$x_1y_1=x_2y_2$
From a table Example	If quotient of y/x is the same (2, 6)(3, 9)(4, 12)	If product of xy is the same (2, 6)(3, 4)(6, 1)

Chapter5: Graphing linear equations and inequalities in two variables and writing linear equations in different forms.

- What are we going to learn about Linear Equations and Inequalities Equations forms and graphing?
  - Slope definition
  - Slope formula
  - Positive slope
  - Negative slope
  - Graphing linear equations
  - Graphing linear inequalities and shading using test point
  - Perpendicular lines slope and equation
  - Parallel lines slope and equation
  - Graphing using slopes
  - Horizontal line slope and equation
  - Vertical line Slope and equation
  - Point slope form
  - Standard form
  - Slope intercept form
  - Changing forms of linear equations
  - x and y intercepts

71. In how many forms can the equation of a line be written?

The equations of <u>lines</u> can be written in three forms:
- Slope-Intercept form: $y=mx+b$
- Point-Slope Form: $y-y_1=m(x-x_1)$
- Standard Form: $Ax+By=C$

72. What is the definition of slope?

Slope is defined as the steepness of a line and equals "the vertical change over the horizontal change".

73. What are other definitions of slope?

$$\text{Slope} = \frac{Rise}{Run} = \frac{Change\ in\ y}{Change\ in\ x}$$

74. What does the slope of a line mean?

Slope of a line means its incline.

Example: If the slope of a line is ½ it means the ratio of the vertical change to horizontal change is 1:2

75. What is the formula to find slope, given two points?

If (x_1, y_1) and (x_2, y_2) are two different points on a line, then the slope of the line is
m = $(y_2-y_1)/(x_2-x_1)$

Picture19: Slope

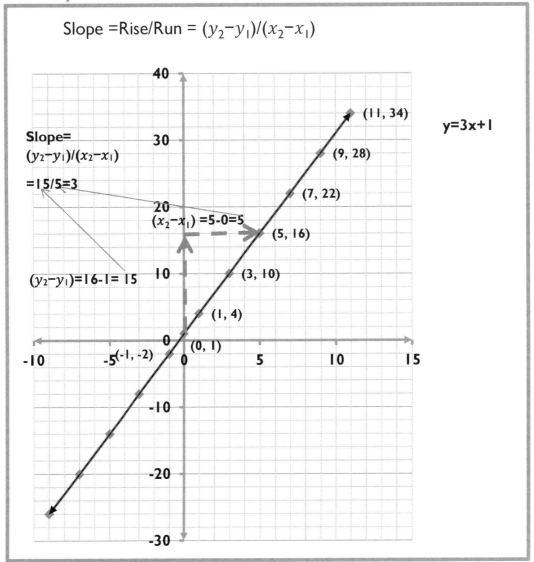

76. **How do you find the slope from a graph and which two points do you pick to find the slope of a line given its graph?**

Pick any two points from the graph and use the slope formula or rise/run. You can pick any two coordinate points on the graph to find the slope. You will get the same value for its slope.

Picture20:Slope

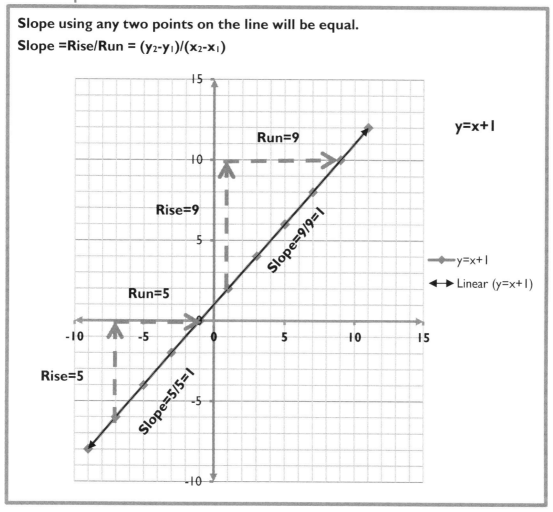

Slope using any two points on the line will be equal.

Slope =Rise/Run = $(y_2-y_1)/(x_2-x_1)$

77. What is a positive slope?

Upward slope from left to right is positive. As "x" increases "y" increases, the graph shows an upward trend.

Example: $y=3x+1$

Solution: The slope is positive 3. This means that every point moves up 3 units for every one unit right.

Picture21: Positive Slope

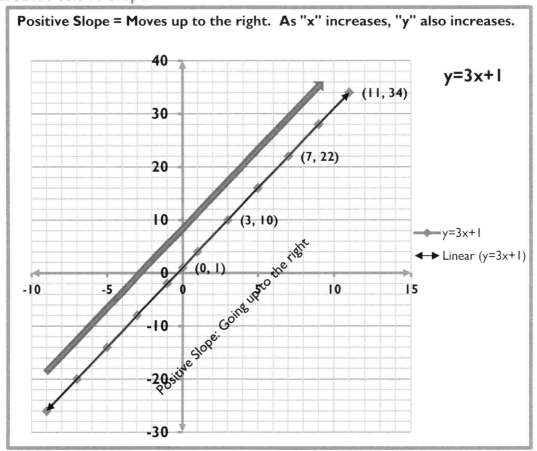

78. What is the slope of a line used for?

The slope can be used to find equations of lines or the relationship between two variables.

79. What is negative slope?

Downward slope from left to right is negative. As "x" increases, "y" decreases. The graph shows a downward trend.

Example: y=-3x+1

Solution: The slope is negative 3. This means every point moves down 3 units for every one unit moved to the right.

Picture22: Negative Slope

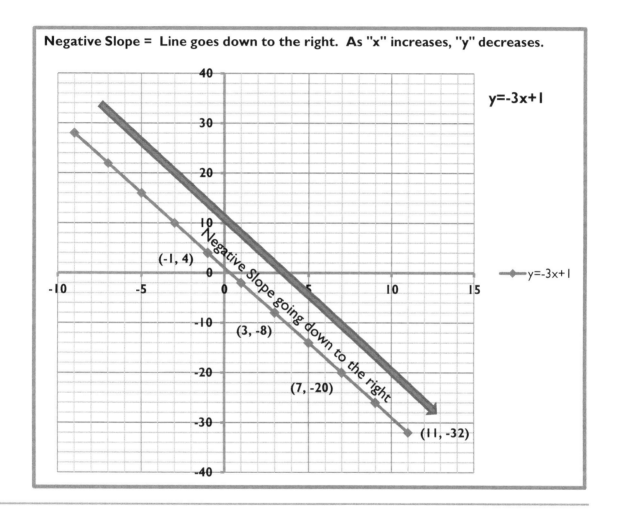

80. When comparing two lines, which slope is higher?

The steeper line has a higher slope. The slope of a line increases as the line becomes steeper.

Picture23: Steeper line has higher slope

As a line becomes steeper its slope increases. A steeper line has a higher slope compared to a flatter line.

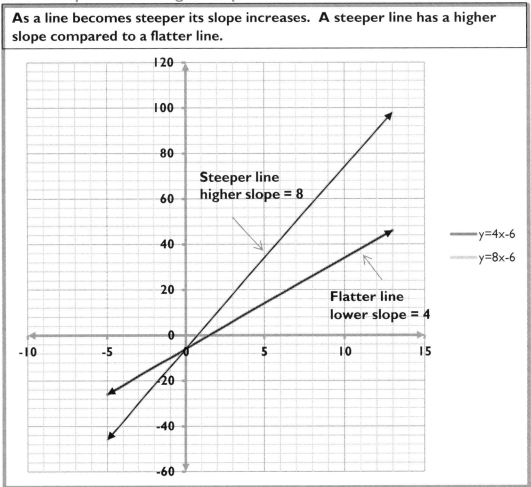

81. What is the slope of a vertical line?

Slope of a vertical line is undefined since "x" does not change. Difference of x's, $x_2-x_1=0$.
Since $m= (y_2-y_1)/(x_2-x_1) = (y_2-y_1)/0 =$ Any number/0 = undefined.

Picture24: Slope of a vertical line

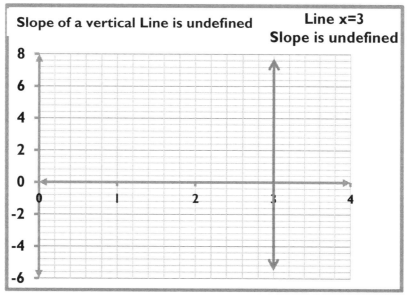

82. What is the slope of a horizontal line?

Slope of a horizontal line is zero. "y" remains the same for all "x". "y" does not change. This means $(y_2-y_1)=0$. Since $m= (y_2-y_1)/(x_2-x_1) = 0/(x_2-x_1) = 0$

Picture25: Slope of a horizontal line

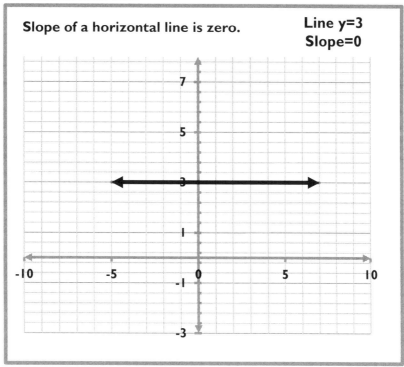

83. How are the slopes of parallel lines related?

Parallel lines have the same slope. $m_1 = m_2$

Picture26: Parallel Lines Slopes

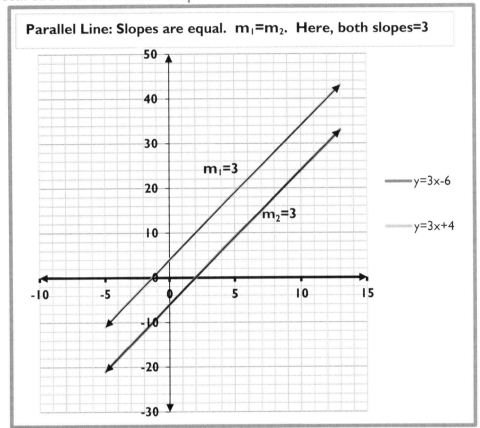

84. How are slopes of perpendicular lines related?

- Perpendicular lines have inverse reciprocal slopes
- When you mutilply the slopes of perpendicular lines, the product of slopes = -1
- Formula to find the perpendicular slope $m_2 = -1/m_1$
- Or simply flip the sign and the number
- Perpendicular slope of 4 is -1/4, Perpendicular slope of -3/5 is +5/3, Perpendicular slope of 5 is -1/5

Picture27: Perpendicular Lines Slopes

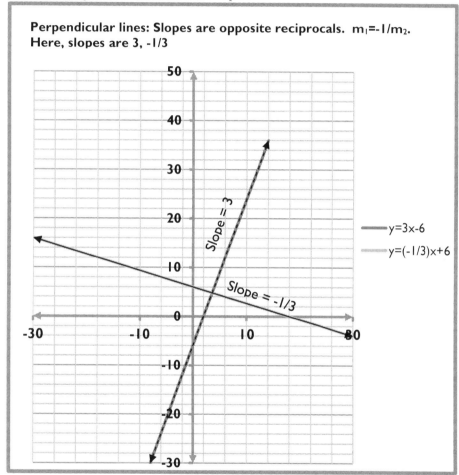

Perpendicular lines: Slopes are opposite reciprocals. $m_1 = -1/m_2$.
Here, slopes are 3, -1/3

85. How do you find the x-intercept and the y-intercept of a line?

To find the x-intercept plug-in y = 0 in the original equation, and solve for "x". To find the y-intercept of a line plug-in x=0 in the original equation and solve for "y".

Example: Find the "x" and "y" intercepts of 5x-6y = 30

Solution: To find the y-intercept of a line plug-in x=0 in the original equation and solve for "y".

5(0)-6y=30	(Plug in x = 0)
0-6y=30	(Divide by -6 on both sides to isolate "y")
y=-5	(y intercept is (0,-5))

To find the x-intercept of a line plug-in y=0 in the original equation and solve for "x".

5x-6(0)=30	(Plug in y = 0)
5x-0=30	(Divide by 5 on both sides to isolate "x")
x=6	(x-intercept is (6,0))

86. What are x and y intercepts?

Intercepts are points at which the graph crosses the x-axis and y-axis.

Picture28: x and y intercepts

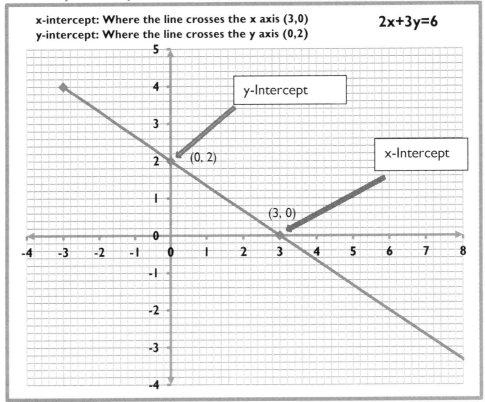

87. How do you graph a linear equation y=mx+b?

Step1) Graph the y-intercept (0,b) on the <u>y-axis</u>.

Step2) Count the slope "m" as rise over run and go up and over. Use the numerator of the slope to go up and the denominator to go right. Then mark the second point. If slope is a whole number use 1 as the denominator. Repeat this procedure if you need more points.

Step 3) Join the two points and extend the line in both directions with arrows.

(Note: Easy way to remember YRRJ(Y-Intercept, Rise, Run, Join))

(If the slope is negative in step 2, go down and right.)

Picture29: Graphing linear equations

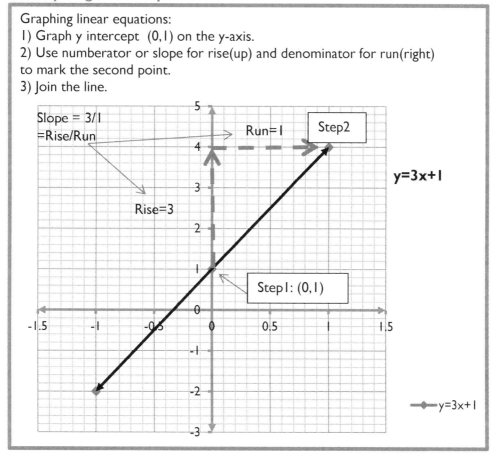

Graphing linear equations:
1) Graph y intercept (0,1) on the y-axis.
2) Use numberator or slope for rise(up) and denominator for run(right) to mark the second point.
3) Join the line.

88. How do you find the equation of a line given the graph?
Method I
Step1) Find the slope of the line using Rise/Run or two points at intersections m=rise/run
Step2) Find the y-intercept
Step3) y=(slope)x+(y-intercept) gives the equation of the line

Picture 30: Equation of the line from the graph

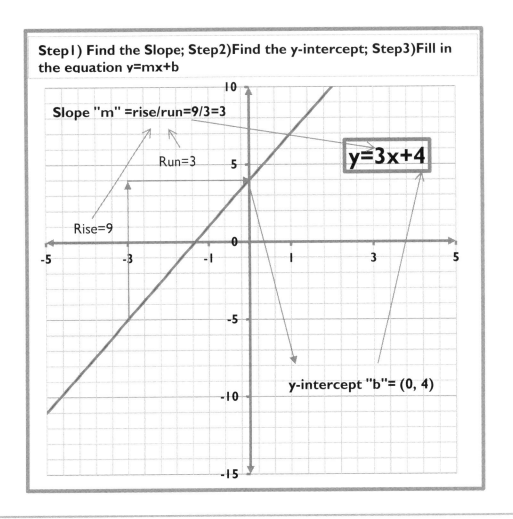

Method II (An example is discussed later in this chapter)
Step1) Pick any two points from the line (x_1, y_1) (x_2, y_2). Find the slope of the line using
$m = (y_2 - y_1)/ (x_2 - x_1)$
Step 2) Using the point-slope equation find the equation of the line
$y -(y_1) = m(x - (x_1))$

89. How do you graph a <u>linear inequality</u> in two variables x and y?
Follow the same steps as graphing a linear equation then add another step for shading in the end.

Step1) Graph the **y-intercept on the y-axis**.

Step2) Use the numerator of the slope to go up and the denominator to go right. In other words, count the **slope as rise over run** and go up and over. Then mark the second point. If slope is a whole number use 1 as the denominator.

Step3) **Join the two points** and extend the line in both directions with arrows. The line is **solid (which means included)** for inequalities with less than or equal to and greater than or equal to(≤, ≥). The line is dashed for inequalities less than or greater than(<, >)

Step4) **Shade the region** which is less than or greater than depending on the question. This is done **using a test point** which is not on the line and plug it into the inequality to see if it is true or false. If true shade on the side where the point is included.

Example: Graph: **y>3x+1**

Picture31: Linear Inequality Graph

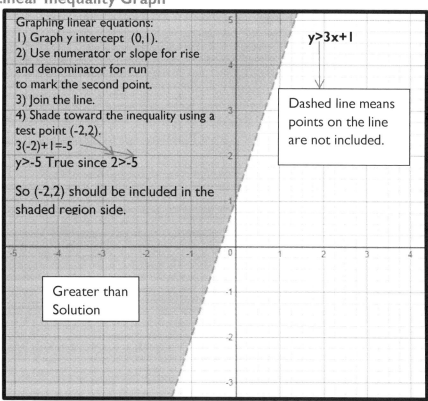

90. To graph an inequality when do you use solid line/dashed lines?
- Solid line is used for included inequalities like <u>greater than and equal to</u> and <u>less than and equal to</u>. ≤, ≥

- Dashed line is used for inequalities that do not include the line such as <u>greater than</u> and <u>less than</u>. <, >

91. Which side of the line do you shade for inequalities?
Inequalities have shaded regions as solutions.

- Greater than is normally above the line or right of it.
- Less than is normally below the line or to the left of it.
- Use a test point such as (0,0) to check if it makes the inequality true or false. If it is true then that point is included in the shaded region. If it is false shade the other side. If (0,0) falls on the line then pick a different point.

92. Where does the greater than region lie for a vertical line?
The greater than region lies to the right of the line for a vertical line.

93. Where does the less than region lie for a vertical line?
The greater than regions lies to the left of the line for a vertical line.

94. Where does the greater than region lie for a horizontal line?
The greater than region lies above the line for the horizontal line.

95. Where does the less than region lie for a horizontal line?
The less than region lies below the line for the horizontal line.

96. What is the slope intercept form:
The slope intercept form of a linear equation is y = (m) x + (b)
where m is the slope and b is the y-intercept.
<u>The slope intercept</u> form is used if the slope "m" and the y intercept (0, b) are known.
Example: Find the equation of a line with slope -2 and y intercept (0, 3)

$$y = -2\,x + 3$$

97. What is the point-slope form?
The point slope form is $y - (y_1) = m\,(x - (x_1))$.

It is useful to find the equation of a line if the slope "m" and a point (x_1, y_1) through which the line passes are known.

Example: Find the equation of a line that passes through the point (5, 7) and has a slope of − 3 in point slope form.

Solution: *y - 7 = -3 (x - 5)*

---

98. **What is the standard form of a linear equation?**

Standard form equation of a line: ***A*** *x* + ***B*** *y* = ***C***, where A, B and C are integer numbers.

"x" and "y" terms are on the left side and the constant is on the right side of the equation. The standard form cannot have any fractions and "A" has to be positive.

Example: Standard form equation of a line:

$$2x - 5y = 8$$

(Note: x and y terms are on the left side and there are no fractions and the coefficient of "x" is a positive integer.)

---

99. **What is the equation of a vertical line?**

Equation of a vertical line is of the form "**x = k**", where k is a constant. Why is it so? Since the slope of a vertical line is undefined there is no "y" term.

Example: The equation of a vertical line that passes through the point (3, -5) may be written as follows: (Hint – Vertical line write "x = x value")

x = 3

Picture32: Vertical Line Graph

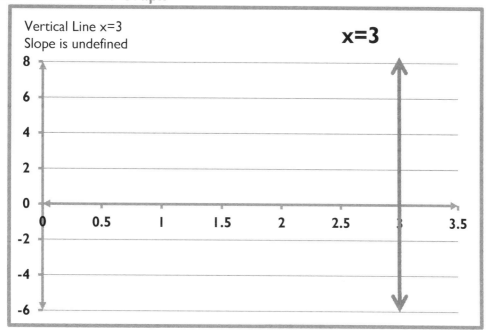

100.   **How do you find the equation of a horizontal line?**

Equation of a horizontal line: $y = k$, where k is a constant. Since the slope of a horizontal line is zero, there is no "x" term.

Example: The equation of a horizontal line that passes through the point (-2, 3) may be written as follows: (Hint – Horizontal line write "y = y value")

$y = 3$

Picture33: Horizontal line Graph

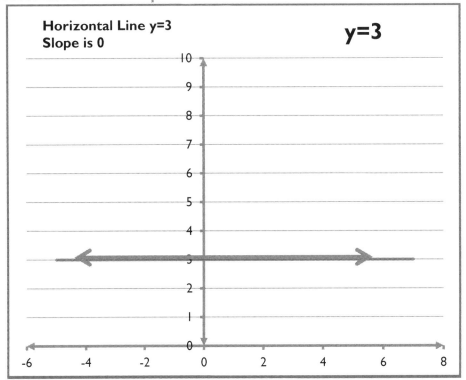

101.   How do you graph special inequalities?

Special inequalities are graphed as vertical or horizontal lines and shaded accordingly.

Picture34: Horizontal line inequality Graph

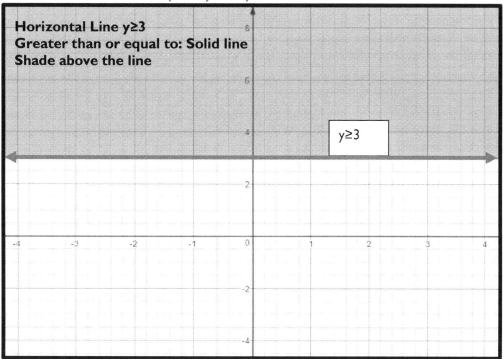

Picture35: Vertical line inequality graph

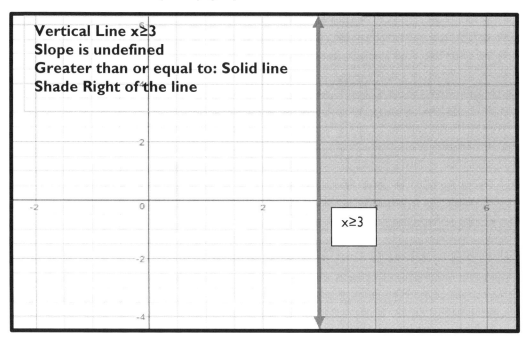

102.   How is the point-slope form of the linear equation defined?

The "point-slope" form is $y - (y_1) = m(x - (x_1))$

where a point (x_1, y_1) and the slope "m" are given. You plug in the x_1, y_1 and m values. Do not plug in values for "x" and "y".

Example: Find the equation of the straight line that has slope $m = 3$ and passes through the point $(-1, -6)$.

Solution: *Plug in* $m = 3$, $x_1 = -1$, and $y_1 = -6$ into the point-slope form, and solve for "y".

$y - (y_1) = m(x - (x_1))$

$y - (-6) = (3)(x - (-1))$	(Plug in given numbers)
$y + 6 = 3(x + 1)$	(Simplify)
$y + 6 = 3x + 3$	(Distribute)
$y = 3x + 3 - 6$	(Subtract 6 on both sides)
$y = 3x - 3$	(Final answer)

103.   How do you find the equation of a line using the point-slope form and the slope-intercept form given two points it passes through?

To find the equation of a line given two points

First, find the slope using the slope "m" formula

$$m = (y_2 - y_1)/(x_2 - x_1)$$

Then use the point-slope equation and plug in m, x_1, y_1 to get an equation in y and x.

$$y - y_1 = m(x - x_1)$$

Example: Find the equation of the line that passes through the points (1, 2) and (−2, 4).

Solution : $x_1 = 1$, $y_1 = 2$, $x_2 = -2$, $y_2 = 4$, Given two points, first find the slope:

m = $(y_2 - y_1)/(x_2 - x_1)$

m = (4-2)/(-2-1) = 2/-3 = -2/3

Then use either point as the (x_1, y_1), along with this slope just calculated, and plug in to the point-slope form. Using (−2, 4) as the (x_1, y_1):

$y - y_1 = m(x - x_1)$

$y - (4) = (-2/3)(x - (-2))$	(Plug in given numbers)
$y - 4 = (-2/3)(x + 2)$	(Simplify signs)
$y - 4 = (-2/3)x - 4/3$	(Distributing the (-2/3) on the RHS)
$y = (-2/3)x - 4/3 + 4$	(Bringing the -4 to right side makes it +4)
$y = (-2/3)x - 4/3 + 12/3$	(Convert 4 to fraction 12/3)
$y = (-2/3)x + 8/3$	(Final answer)

104. **How do you change an equation from the standard form Ax+By=C to Slope Intercept form y=mx+b?**

Starting with the standard form Ax+By=C, our goal is to isolate "y" on one side.

Step 1) First you want to move the Ax term to the opposite side of the equation, by either adding or subtracting it. Opposite operation makes terms move to the other side of the equation. At this point your equation will be set up like this

By = -Ax + C.

Step 2) Isolate "y" by dividing ALL terms by B.

By/B = - Ax/B + C/B.

Step 3) B's cancel on the left side. Reduce the terms on the right side

y = - Ax/B + C/B.

This is the slope-intercept form y = mx+b.

Example: *Change from standard to slope intercept form by solving for "y"*

8x + 4y = 16

Solution:

8x + 4y = 16	(Transpose 8x to the right side to isolate "y")
4y = -8x + 16	(Divide all terms by 4 to islolate "y")
y = -2x + 4	(Slope-intercept form where slope=-2 and y-intercept=(0,4))

---

105. **How do you find the equation of the line parallel to a linear graph and that passes through a given point?**

To find the equation of a line parallel to a given line and passing through a given point, use point slope equation, parallel or same slope and given point.

Example: Find the equation of the line parallel to the graph of 3x-y=5, that passes through the point (-1,4)?

Solution: First find the slope of the given line: 3x-y=5 by isolating "y"

y = 3x - 5

Slope = 3

The slope of the new line is equal to parallel line's slope so, m=3 & point given $(x_1, y_1) = (-1,4)$

Equation of a line = $y - y_1 = m (x - x_1)$

y − 4 = 3(x- (-1))

Changing the equation to slope intercept form: Distribute the right side and isolate "y".

y-4 = 3x+3

y=3x+7

106.   **How do you find the equation of the line perpendicular to a linear graph that passes through a given point?**

To find the equation of a line perpendicular to a given line and passing through a given point, use point-slope equation with perpendicular or opposite reciprocal slope and given point.

Example: How do you find the equation of the line perpendicular to a linear graph of 3x-y=5, that passes through the point (-1,4)?

Solution: First find the slope of the given line by isolating "y"

y = 3x - 5; slope = 3, x_1=-1, y_1=4

The slope of the new perpendicular line equals the opposite reciprocal of 3 = -1/3

Now plug m=-1/3 into the point slope equation "$y - y_1 = m (x - x_1)$"

y – 4 = -1/3(x- (-1))

(Since the form not mentioned we can leave the equation in point-slope form)

---

107.   **How do you change an equation from point slope form**

"$y - y_1 = m (x - x_1)$" to slope intercept form "y=mx+b"?

Distribute the right side, then isolate "y" and combine like terms. It seems like an easy transformation but common mistakes are made when there are negatives and fractions.

Example: y – 4 = -1/3(x- (-1))

Solution:

Method I:

First multiply out the inside of the parenthesis.

y – 4 = (-1/3) (x + 1))	(Distribute with all signs)
y - 4 = $-\frac{1}{3}$x - $\frac{1}{3}$	(Multiply)
y = $\frac{-1}{3}$x + $\frac{11}{3}$	(Final answer)

Method II:

y – 4 = -1/3(x- (-1))	(Point-Slope Form of this equation)
3(y-4)= -1(x+1)	(Bring the denominator of the slope to distribute to the left side)
3y-12=-x-1	(Muliply the numerator of the slope to the right side)
3y= - x+11	(Isolate "y")
y= - $\frac{1}{3}$x+$\frac{11}{3}$	(Slope-Intercept form of this equation)

---

108.   **If a line passes through three points (x_1, y_1), (x_2, y_2), (x_3, y_3) then the slopes through any two points are equal.**

Hence, $(y_3-y_2)/(x_3-x_2) = (y_2-y_1)/(x_2-x_1) = (y_1-y_3)/(x_1-x_3)$

Example: If a line passes through (1,2)(3,4)(5,6), then the slope from any two pair of points are equal.

Solution: Slope of $(1,2)(3,4) = (4-2)/(3-1) = 2/2 = 1$
                       Slope of $(3,4)(5,6) = (6-4)/(5-3) = 2/2 = 1$
                       Slope of $(1,2)(5,6) = (6-2)/(5-1) = 4/4 = 1$. All slopes are equal.

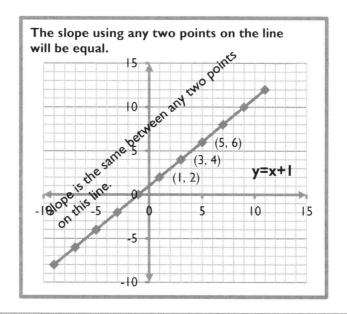

109.   **How do you find the rule for a function from the given data table?**
To find the rule first check if it's a linear relationship by dividing difference of y's over difference of x's. Then point slope equation is used to find the rule.
Example: Find the function rule for the following table.

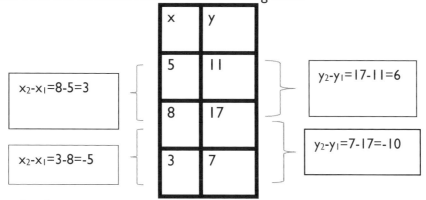

Solution: To find the rule, first check if the function is linear.
            Pick any two "ys" and subtract the y's and then subtract the corresponding x's.
            Quotient of the two, Difference of y's/Difference of x's have to be equal.
            $(y_2-y_1)/(x_2-x_1) = 6/3 = 2$; $(y_2-y_1)/(x_2-x_1) = -10/-5 = 2$. This is the slope. m=2
            This is a linear function. To find the equation, use point slope,
            "$y - y_1 = m (x - x_1)$"
            $y-11=2(x-5)$ (Here we are using the point (5,11) from the table)
            $y=2x+1$

110. **How do you find the terms of a series given the function?**

Plug in numbers for n in f(n). n=1, n=2, n=3 depending on how many tems you need to find.

Example: Find the first 4 terms of the series $f(n)=2n^3-1$

$n=1, f(1)=2(1)^3-1=2-1=1$

$n=2, f(2)=2(2)^3-1=16-1=15$

$n=3, f(3)=2(3)^3-1=54-1=53$

$n=4, f(4)=2(4)^3-1=128-1=127$

The first 4 terms of the series are: 1, 15, 53, 127

Arithmetic Series

111. **What is an arithmetic series?**

An arithmetic series is a number series or a list in which each term differs from the previous term by a constant difference "d". It means you add or subtract the same number every time to get the next term.

Example: 2, 7, 12, 17, 22, 17...Here the common difference "d" is +5, the first term "a_1" is 2.

112. **How do you find the common difference of an arithmetic series?**

Common difference "d" is found by difference in consecutive terms.

$d = a_{n+1} - a_n$

If the consecutive terms are not given, then a formula to find the common difference given the first and nth term would be derived as:

$d = (a_n - a_1)/(n-1)$

113. **How do you find the explicit formula for nth term or the rule for an arithmetic series?**

If the first term of an arithmetic series is the number "a_1" and the common difference is "d", then the nth term of an arithmetic series can be found by the formula:

$a_n = a_1 + (n-1)d$

Example: If the first 3 terms in an arithmetic series are 3,7,11 then what is the 15th term?

Solution: The first term is $a_1 = 3$, and the common difference is d = 4 and n=15.

$a_n = a_1 + (n - 1)d$

$a_n=3+(15-1)4$

$a_{15}= 3 +56$

$a_{15}= 59$

114.   **How do you find the recursive formula for nth term or the rule for an arithmetic series?**

If the first term of an arithmetic series is the number "a_1" and the common difference is "d", then the nth term of an arithmetic series can be found by the recursive formula:

$a_n = a_{n-1} + d$, **given a_1 which means the nth term is given by the previous term plus the common difference. Also the first term has to be defined.**

Example: If the first 3 terms in an arithmetic series are 3,7,11 then what is the 5th term?

Solution: The first term is $a_1 = 3$, and the common difference is d = 4 and n=15.

$a_n = a_{n-1} + d$ here $a_n = a_{n-1} + 4$, $a_1 = 3$

$a_2 = a_1 + d = 3+4=9$

$a_3 = a_2 + d = 9+4=13$

$a_4 = a_3 + d = 13+4=17$

$a_5 = a_4 + d = 17+4=21$

115.   **How do you find the total sum of all terms of an arithmetic series?**

If the first term of an arithmetic series is "a_1" and the common difference is "d", the sum of n terms of a arithmetic series can be found by the formula

$S = \frac{n}{2}[2a_1 + (n-1)d]$ **or** $S = \frac{n}{2}[a_1 + a_n]$ where tn is the last term

Example: If the first 3 terms in an arithmetic series are 8, 5, and 2 then what is the sum of the first 20 terms?

Solution: a_1=8, d=-3

$S = \frac{n}{2}[2a_1 + (n-1)d]$

$S_{20} = (20/2)(2 \times 8 + (20 - 1) \times (-3))$

$= 10(16 - 57)$

$=10(-41)$

$=-410$

Geometric Series

116.   **What is a geometric series/sequence?**

A geometric series is a number series or a list in which each term is multiplied by a constant number to find the next term. The ratio of a term to its previous term is constant. It means you multiply by the same number or fraction every time to get the next term.

Example: 2, 4, 8, 16, 32, 64...

Here the common ratio is 2 and the first term is 2.

117.   How do you find the common ratio of a geometric series?

The common ratio "r" of a geometric series is found by dividing any term by its preceding term.

$r = a_{n+1}/a_n$

Example: r = Second term/first term a_2/a_1

---

118.   How do you find the formula or rule for a geometric series?

If the first term of an geometric series is the number "a_1" and the common ratio is "r", then the nth term "a_n" of an geometric term can be found by the formula

$a_n = a_1 r^{n-1}$

Example: If the first 3 terms in an geometric series are 1,3, and 9 then what is the 6th term?

Solution: The first term is $a_1 = 1$, and the common ratio is r = 3 and n=6.

$a_n = a_1 r^{n-1}$

$a_6 = 1.(3)^{6-1}$

$a_6 = 3^5$

$a_6 = 243$

---

119.   How do you find the total sum of all terms of a geometric series?

If the first term of an geometric series is "a_1" and the common ratio is "r", the sum of n terms of the geometric series can be found by the formula

$S_n = a_1 (1- r^n)/(1-r)$ if r<1

$S_n = a_1 (r^n-1)/(r-1)$ if r>1

$S_n = a_1/(1-r)$ for infinite terms and r<1

Example: If the first 3 terms in a geometric series are 2,4,8 then what is the sum of the first 10 terms?

Solution: a_1=2, r=4/2=2

$S_n = a_1 (r^n-1)/(r-1)$ if r>1

$S_{10} = 2(2^{10}-1)/(2-1)$ if r>1

$S_{10} = 2(1024-1/1) = S_{10} = 2046$

---

120.   How do you evaluate a geometric series of the summation form?

Example: $$\sum_{n=1}^{31} 2(3/2)^{n-1}$$

Solution: The sigma symbol stands for the "sum of". The sum of all the values obtained from evaluating the function at all integer values of n from 1 to 31.

When n = 1, the function = $2(3/2)^1 = 3$

When n = 31, the function = $2(3/2)^{31}$

The easy way to evaluate is to use the Sum formula. Here a_1=2, r=3/2=1.5, n=31,

$S_n = a_1 (r^n-1)/(r-1)$ if r>1

$S_n = 2 (1.5^{31}-1)/(1.5-1)$

$S_n = 1150502.36$

121.   How do you find the midpoint between two given points?

The midpoint of a segment is the point that divides the segment into two congruent pieces. The midpoint of the segment that joins points (x_1, y_1) and (x_2, y_2) is the point $\left(\dfrac{x_1 + x_2}{2}, \dfrac{y_1 + y_2}{2} \right)$.

To find the midpoint of the line joining (x_1, y_1) and (x_2, y_2), find the arithmetic average of the two"x"values and average of the two "y" values(add and divide by 2).

Example: Find the midpoint of the line segment with the following end points (4, 6) and (2, 8)

Solution: First write down $x_1=4$, $y_1=6$; $x_2=2$, $y_2=8$

Using the above formula $(x_1+x_2)/2$, $(y_1+y_2)/2$

= $((4+2)/2, (6+8)/2)$

= $(6/2, 14/2)$

= $(3, 7)$

Picture36: Midpoint Picture

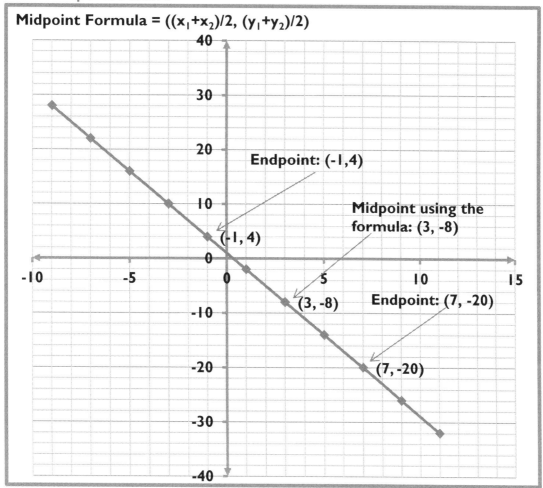

122.   How do you find the distance between two given points on a graph?

The distance formula to find the distance between two given points is:

$$d = \sqrt{(x_2 - x_1)^2 + (y_2 - y_1)^2}$$

Picture 37: Distance between two points

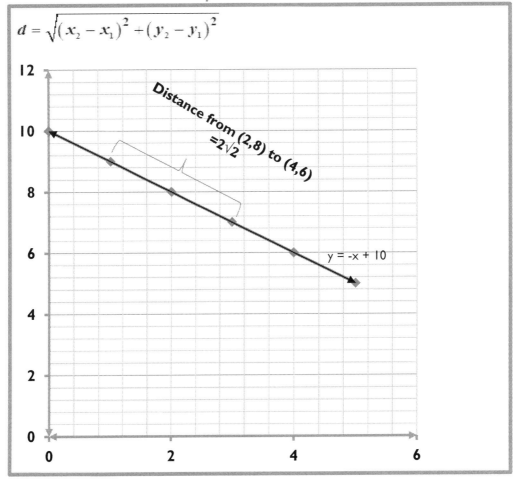

Example: Find the distance between the two points (4, 6) and (2, 8)

Solution: Here $x_1=4$, $y_1=6$, $x_2=2$, $y_2=8$

Now use the distance formula

$$d = \sqrt{(x_2 - x_1)^2 + (y_2 - y_1)^2}$$

Plug in numbers to find

$$d = \sqrt{(2-4)^2 + (8-6)^2}$$
$$= \sqrt{(-2)^2 + (2)^2}$$
$$= \sqrt{4+4} = \sqrt{8} = 2\sqrt{2} \text{ units}$$

123.   How do you solve <u>systems of linear inequalities</u> in two variables "x" and "y" using the graphing method?

Follow the same steps as graphing of linear inequalities and then add another step in the end. Y/RR/DS/AB: Y-intercept/Rise over Run/Dashed or Solid/Above or Below

Graph both inequalities separately. Shade the regions then find the intersection of the shaded regions.

Step1) Graph the y-intercept on the y-axis.

y –intercept =

Step2) Count the slope as rise over run and go up and over. Use the numerator of the slope to go up and the denominator to go right. Then mark the second point. If it is a whole number use 1 as the denominator.

Run=

Rise =

Slope = Rise /Run =

Step 3) Join the two points and extend the line in both directions with arrows. The line is solid (which means included) for inequalities that contain <u>less than or equal to</u> or <u>greater than or equal to</u>. The line is dashed for less than or greater than inequalities.

Dashed or Solid Line?

Step4) Shade the region which is less than or greater than depending on the question. Use a test point which is not on the line and plug it into the inequality to see if it is true or false. If true shade that side.

Test Point?

Shade Above/Below or Right/Left?

Step5) Solution is the area of intersection of both the shaded regions.

Example: Solve y>-3x+10 and y<2x using graphing method

Y/RR/DS/AB: Y-intercept/Rise over Run/Dashed or Solid/Above or Below

Picture38: Linear Inequality Graph

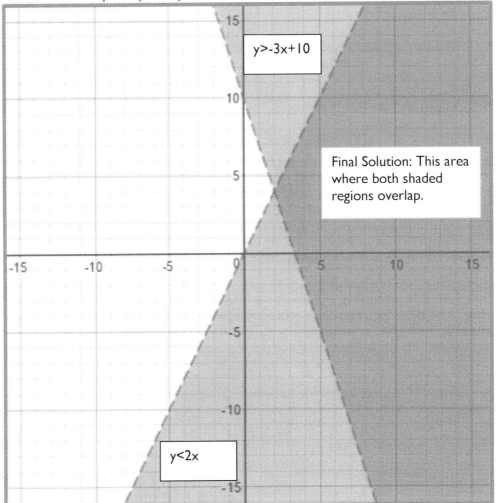

y>-3x+10

Final Solution: This area where both shaded regions overlap.

y<2x

124.   How do you write a <u>system of linear inequalities</u> in two variables "x" and "y" given a graph?

To find a system of linear inequalities follow the same steps as graphing of linear inequalities.

Y/RR/DS/AB: Y-intercept/Rise over Run/Dashed or Solid/Above or Below

Picture39: Writing Linear Inequality System from the Graph

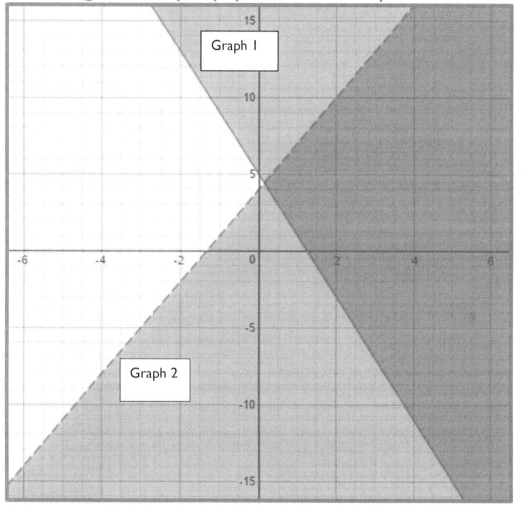

© Vaishali Patil

First Graph

Step1) Find the y-intercept on the y-axis.

y –intercept of first graph = (0,5)

Step2) Find the slope as rise over run and go up/down and over. Use the numerator of the slope to go up and the denominator to go right. Then find the second point. If the slope is a whole number use 1 as the denominator.

Slope of the first graph = Rise /Run =-4/1 where Rise = -4; Run= 1

Step 3)Find the inequality of the first line

Dashed or Solid Line? First line is a Solid line so it's also going to be "equal to"

Step4) Location of the shaded region?

Shade Above/Below or Right/Left? Above so "Greater than"

Now write the inequality   **y ≥ -4x+5**

Second Graph

Step1) Find the y-intercept on the y-axis.

y –intercept of first graph = (0,4)

Step2) Find the slope as rise over run and go up/down and over. Use the numerator of the slope to go up and the denominator to go right. Then find the second point. If it is a whole number use 1 as the denominator.

Slope of the first graph = Rise /Run =3/1; Here Rise = 3; Run= 1

Step 3)Find the inequality of second line

Dashed or Solid Line? Dashed so does not include the line

Step4) Which side is the shaded region?

Shade Above/Below or Right/Left? Below so "Less than"

Now write the inequality   **y < 3x+4**

The system $\begin{cases} y \geq -4x+5 \\ y < 3x+4 \end{cases}$

---

125. **How do you find the y-intercept of the line perpendicular to a given line and passing through a given point?**

Find the equation of the line given the perpendicular slope and a point using point-slope and change it to slope intercept form. Then find the y-intercept.

Example: Find the y intercept of the line perpendicular to y=3x+4 and passing through the point (1, 2).

Solution: This is a simple question but worded differently, it means we have to find the equation first and then the y-intercept. We have to find the equation of a line given perpendicular-slope and a point. Then find its y-intercept.

y = 3x + 4. Slope of given line = 3

Slope of the new perpendicular line, Perpendicular slope = -1/3, Here x_1=1, y_1=2

Now plug into point slope equation "y – y_1 = m (x – x_1)"

$y - 2 = -\frac{1}{3}(x- (1))$

$y - 2 = -\frac{1}{3}x + \frac{1}{3}$

$y = -\frac{1}{3}x + \frac{7}{3}$

So the y-intercept of the line will be $(0, \frac{7}{3})$

Chapter 6: Systems of Equations

- What are we going to learn in Systems of Equations?
    - Types of systems
    - Different methods of solving systems
    - Solve by Addition/Elimination Method
    - Solve by Substitution
    - Solve by Graphing
    - System of 3 equations

126.   What is a system of equations?

A combination of two or more equations that are simultaneously true for two or more variables. These are also known as simultaneous equations.

Example: This is a system of equations in "x" and "y"

$$\begin{cases} x = y + 3 \\ y + 3x = 1 \end{cases}$$

127.   How do you solve a system of equations?

There are three methods to solve a system of equations:

- Solving by Substitution
- Solving by Elimination
- Solving by Graphing

128.   How do you solve a system of equations by substitution method?

Given a system of equations in variables "x" and "y"

$$\begin{cases} ax+by=c \quad \text{(i)} \\ dx+ey=f \quad \text{(ii)} \end{cases}$$

Step 1)Using equation (i) isolate "x".*(Same can be done with "y" or second equation)*

Step 2) Substitute this value of "x" into the equation (ii). This gives an equation entirely in variable "y".

Step 3) Solve for "y".

Step 4) Substitute the "y" value back in the first equation to solve for "x".

Step 4) Write the solution as an ordered pair.

Step 5) Plug in the solution in the original equations to check.

In short: Isolate, Substitute, Solve, Substitute, Check (ISSSC)

Example: Solve a system of equations by substitution.

$$\begin{cases} x = y + 3 \\ y + 3x = 1 \end{cases}$$

Solution: x = $\boxed{y + 3}$

$$y + \quad 3x \quad = 1$$

Step 1) The first equation is already solved for "x".

Step 2) Substitute (y + 3) in for "x" in the second equation.

It becomes y + 3(y + 3) = 1

Step 3) Solve for "y".

y + 3y + 9 = 1

4y = -8

y = -2

Step 4) Solve for "x"

Substitute -2 in for "y" in the first equation to solve for "x".

x = y + 3 becomes

x = -2 + 3

x = 1

Step 5) Write the solution as an ordered pair.

The solution to the system of equations is (1, -2).

Step 6) Plug in the solution in the original equations to check.

1=-2+3 (check)

-2+3(1)=1 (check)

Example: Solve by substitution the following system

$$\begin{cases} 4x + 3y = 1 \\ x = 1 - y \end{cases}$$

Solution: 4x + 3y = 1   (Substituting into this equation)

x = 1 – y   (Isolating from this equation)

Step 1) Isolating "x", "x" is already solved for in the second equation.

x = 1 – y

Step 2) Substitute (1-y) in for "x" in the second equation.

4 (1-y) + 3y = 1

Step 3) Solve for "y".

4 – 4y + 3y =1

4 – y = 1

y = 3

Step 4) Solve for "x"

x = 1 – 3, x = -2

Step 5) Write the solution as an ordered pair (-2, 3)

Step 6) Plug in the solution in the original equations to check.

4(-2)+3(3)=1 (check)

-2=1-3 (check)

129.   **How do you solve a system by Elimination or Addition Method?**

Example: Solve a system of equations by Elimination Method.

$$\begin{cases} 2x + 3y = -1 \\ x - 2y = 17 \end{cases}$$

Solution: The goal here is to eliminate one of the variables by adding the two equations together. This means the coefficients or numbers in front of "x" or "y" in both equations have to be made opposites so that they can cancel each other when added. To do this, one or both equations may have to be multiplied first by a number to get opposite coefficients for one variable. Opposites is the keyword here.

Step 1)
$$\begin{cases} 2x + 3y = -1 \\ x - 2y = 17 \end{cases}$$
           (i)
           (ii)

Make these two numbers coefficients opposites by multiplying equation (ii) throughout by a number.

To eliminate "x" we have to multiply the equation (ii) by -2. Keep equation (i) as is.

$$\begin{cases} 2x + 3y = -1 \\ -2(x - 2y = 17) \end{cases}$$
           (iii)
           (iv)

Step 2) Add the two equations (iii) and (iv) together, eliminate "x". 2x and -2x cancel each other.

$$\begin{cases} 2x + 3y = -1 \\ -2x + 4y = -34 \end{cases}$$
$$+7y = -35$$

Step 3) Solve for y

       y = -5 (Divided both sides by 7)

Step 4) Solve for "x"

       2x + 3(-5) = -1 (Substitute the value of "y" into the equation (i))

       2x - 15 = -1

       2x = 14

       x = 7

Step 5) Write the solution as an ordered pair.

       The solution to the system of equations is (7, -5).

Step 6) Plug in the solution in the original equations to check.

       2(7) + 3(-5) = -1 (check)

       7 - 2(-5) = 17 (check)

130.   **How do you solve a Special Case System of equations with no solution?**

Example: Consider the following system. This can be solved by either substitution or elimination method. Using elimination method,

$$\begin{cases} 4x + 8y = 9 \\ x + 2y = 3 \end{cases}$$

Solution: 4x + 8y = 9 (Substituting into this equation)

$$x = 3 - 2y \text{ (Isolating from this equation)}$$

Step 1) Isolating "x", "x" is already solved for in the second equation.

$$x = 3 - 2y$$

Step 2) Substitute (3-2y) in for "x" in the second equation.

$$4 (3-2y) + 8y = 9$$
$$12 - 8y + 8y = 9$$

Step 3) Solve for y,

$$12 = 9$$

All variables got canceled. And the above statement 12=9 is false so this is a special case of systems with no solution.

---

131.   What is a Special Case Systems with infinite solutions?

When solving a system and all variables cancel and you have a true statement then the system is a special case with infinite solutions that lie on the line given.

---

132.   How do you solve a system of equations by graphing method?

To solve a system by the graphing method, graph each equation and find the point of intersection. Examples are shown below. There can be different kinds of solutions based on the kind of system: One solution, no solution, infinite solutions.

---

133.   What are the different kinds of systems of equations?

The different kinds of systems are:
- Independent: An independent system is a system with only one solution.
- Dependent: A dependent system has the same equation twice(infinite solutions)
- Consistent: A system which has solutions(intersecting lines)
- Inconsistent: A system with no solutions(parallel lines)

---

134.   What is an independent system and how many solutions does it have?

An independent system is a system with only one solution.

In terms of a graph, the two lines intersect each other once. **The slopes are different. y-intercept may or may not be the same.**

Example: $\begin{cases} y=3x-6 \\ y=-2x+4 \end{cases}$

Solution: Independent, x=2, y=0

Picture2: Independent system graph

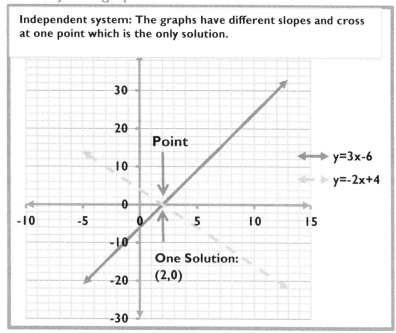

135.   Where is an independent system used?

An independent system is used to solve most practical algebra problems. For example you may be given a Cost and Revenue function and asked to find the breakeven point.

136.   What is a dependent system?

A dependent system is a special case that has the same repeated equation. It has all real number solutions that lie on that line. All points (x, y) on the graph or line are solutions. In terms of the graph it's the same line on itself. **The slopes and y-intercepts are the same.**

Example: Solve $\left\{\begin{array}{l} y=3x-6 \\ 2y=6x-12 \end{array}\right.$ (i)
                                        (ii)

Solution: This is a dependent system, the second equation is the same as first except it is multiplied by 2 throughout.

The solution to this system is **all real number** coordinates that satisfy the equation.

$$y=3x+6$$

Picture3: Dependent system graph

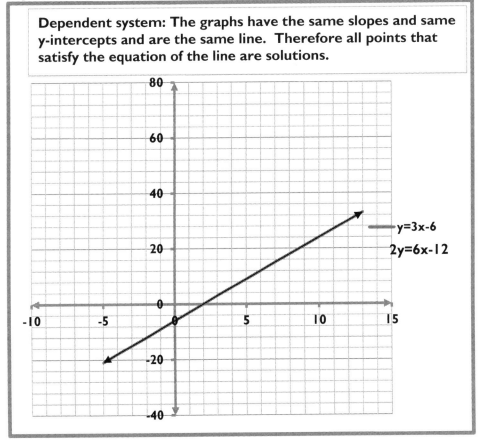

Dependent system: The graphs have the same slopes and same y-intercepts and are the same line. Therefore all points that satisfy the equation of the line are solutions.

$y=3x-6$
$2y=6x-12$

137.   How are the slopes and y-intercepts of the dependent system related?

Slopes of equations of a dependent system are equal; y-intercepts are equal.

138.   **What is an inconsistent system and how many solutions does it have?**

An inconsistent system is when the two equations have **no solution**. Graphically, these are two parallel lines that never meet because they have **the same slopes and different y-intercepts**.

Example: Solve $\begin{cases} y=3x-6 \\ y=3x+4 \end{cases}$

Solution: Algebraically solving, since y's are equal, equate the right sides: 3x-6=3x+4
-6=4. By algebraic method to solve for "y" and we arrive at a false statement which means there is no solution.

These are parallel lines that never meet so the there is no solution.

There is **no ordered pair** that satisfies both equations.

Picture4: Inconsistent system graph

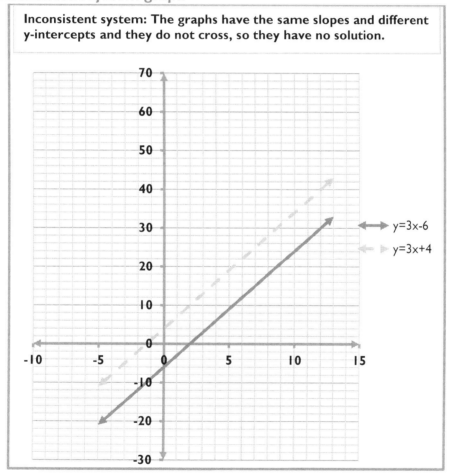

Inconsistent system: The graphs have the same slopes and different y-intercepts and they do not cross, so they have no solution.

y=3x-6

y=3x+4

139.   **How are the slopes and y-intercepts of the inconsistent system related?**

Slopes of inconsistent systems are equal; y-intercepts are different.

140.   How do you solve a system of three equations?

Step1) Eliminate one variable using first two equations

Step2) Eliminate the same variable using the last two equations

Step3) Now you have a resulting system of two equations in two variables.

Step4) Solve the system of two equations using addition or substitution methods.

Step 5) Plug in the values of the two variables into one of the original to find the value of the third variable.

Example: Solve
$$\begin{cases} 3x - 5y + 2z = 17 \\ 4x + y + 4z = 19 \\ 2x - 3y - 3z = -2 \end{cases}$$

Solution: First let's pick a variable here "z" to eliminate from all three equations.

Eliminate z from first two equations so multiply the first equation by -2

$-2(3x - 5y + 2z = 17) = -6x+10y-4z=-34$

Add to second equation

$$\begin{cases} -6x+10y-4z =-34 \\ 4x + y + 4z = 19 \end{cases}$$

Result:-2x+11y   =-15

Now eliminate z from the second and third equations so multiply the second equation by 3 and third equation by 4

$3(4x +y +4z = 19) = 12x+3y+12z=57$

$4(2x - 3y - 3z = -2) = 8x-12y-12z=-8$

$$\begin{cases} 12x+3y+12z=57 \\ 8x-12y-12z =-8 \end{cases}$$

Result:20x-9y   =49

Now use the resulting equations in two variables to solve for "x" and "y".

$$\begin{cases} -2x+11y=-15 \\ 20x-9y = 49 \end{cases}$$

Finally add the two equations so multiply the first equation by 10 to eliminate "x".

$10(-2x+11y=-15)$

$$\begin{cases} -20x+110y=-150 \\ 20x - 9y = 49 \end{cases}$$

$101y=-101$

y=-1

Plug into one of the resulting equations to solve for "x"

$-2x+11(-1)=-15$

$-2x-11=-15$

$-2x=-4$

x=2

Plug in x and y into one of the original equations to solve for "z".

$3x - 5y + 2z = 17$

$3(2)-5(-1) + 2z=17$

$6+5+2z=17$

$2z=6$

z=3

Final answer: x=2, y=-1, z=3 (Plug into another original equations to check.)

Chapter 7: Exponents

- What are we going to learn about Exponents?
  - Product Rule
  - Quotient Rule
  - Power Rule
  - Zero Exponent Rule
  - Reciprocal Power Rule
  - Negative Exponent Rule
  - Fractional Exponents

141. **What is the product rule of exponents?**

Product Rule of exponents states that when multiplying "like" or same variable/bases, **Add the powers** and **multipy the front coefficients**.

$ax^m \cdot bx^n = (a.b) \, x^{m+n}$

Example: $x^8 \cdot x \cdot x^{13}$ (Since base is the same "x", add the exponents)

Solution: $x^{8+1+13} = x^{22}$

Example: $(3x^2)(5x^8)$

Solution: $(3)(5)x^{2+8} = 15x^{10}$ *(MULTIPLY the COEFFICIENTS in front and ADD the POWERS.)*

Example: $(4m^8n^2)(-2mn^4)(5m^4n^3)$

Solution: $(4)(-2)(5)(m^{8+1+4})(n^{2+4+3}) = -40m^{13}n^9$ *(MULTIPLY the COEFFICIENTS in front and ADD the POWERS.)*

142. **What is the power rule of exponents?**

Power rule states that when a power of a variable is raised to another power distribute and **multiply powers** to each coefficient and variable separately.

$(x^m)^n = x^{m \text{ times } n}$

Hint: Power to power, multiply powers.

$(x^m y^m)^n = x^{m.n} y^{m.n}$

Read this hint slowly - (when a monomial is raised to another power, distribute the power to the coefficient separately and each of the variables separately and if the base already has a power then multiply powers when distributing)

Example: $(a^4b^3)^2$

Solution: $a^{4(2)}b^{3(2)} = a^8b^6$

Example: $(-2xy^7z^2)^5$

Solution: $(-2)^5 x^{1(5)} y^{7(5)} z^{2(5)} = -32x^5y^{35}z^{10}$

Example: $(6a^{12}b^7)^2$

Solution: $6^2 a^{24} b^{14} = 36a^{24}b^{14}$

Example: $(-c^5d^2)^5$
Solution: $(-1)^5c^{5(5)}d^{2(5)}=-c^{25}d^{10}$

143.   What is the Quotient Rule of Exponents

Quotient Rule states that when dividing monomials with like bases, **subtract the powers**. $\dfrac{x^m}{x^n} = x^{m-n}$

(Note: To avoid negative exponents try to always subtract higher power minus the lower power. If the denominator is greater then put a place holder 1 in the numerator for the fraction.)

Example: $\dfrac{m^7n^7}{m^4n^{10}}$ (Remember higher power minus lower
                                                for each variable)
Solution: m^{7-4}/n^{10-7}
                m^3/n^3
                m^3/n^3

Example: $\dfrac{a^3b^7}{a^{-5}b^9}$ (Remember higher power minus lower for each variable)
Solution: $a^{3-(-5)}/b^{(9-7)}$
                a^8/b^2
                a^8/b^2

Example: $\dfrac{n^7}{n^{10}}$ (Remember higher power minus lower for each variable)
Solution: $1/n^{10-7}$
                $1/n^3$

144.   What is the zero power rule?

Zero power rule states that any term to <u>the zero power is equal to 1</u>. So if the exponent is zero the monomial reduces to 1.

$$\boxed{x^0 = 1}$$

Example: $(4m^8n^2)(-2mn4)^0$
Solution: In this example the second parenthesis is raised to 0 so all terms inside
        that parenthesis become equal to 1 = $(4m^8n^2)(1) = 4m^8n^2$

145.   What is the exponent of the coefficient?

The exponent of the coefficient depends on what it is raised to, if it is not raised to any number, the exponent is 1.
Example: The exponent of 4 in $4m^8n^2$ is 1, since 4 is not raised to any number.
(Common mistake 8 is assumed an exponent of 4 since 4 is attached to x and exponent of x is 8. This is incorrect. Only x gets the exponent 8.)
Example: The exponent of 4 in $(4m^8n^2)^3$ is going to be three after power rule.

146.   **What is the negative power rule?**

Negative power rule states that if a variable "x" has a negative power "-n" take the **reciprocal** of the variable to make the power positive "n".

If "x" has a negative power in the denominator, then move the variable to the numerator and switch the power sign to positive.

$$\frac{1}{x^{-n}} = x^n \qquad \text{(x goes up and n becomes positive)}$$

If "x" has a negative power in the numerator, then move the variable to the denominator and switch the power sign to positive.

Note: After moving variables to the denominator if there are no terms in the numerator add a one for placeholder.

$$x^{-n} = \frac{1}{x^n} \qquad \text{(x goes down and n becomes positive)}$$

Another way of writing this rule:

Example: Simplify $3x^{-4}$

Solution: 3 stays in its place and we will move only the variable with a negative exponent to the denominator. Here the "x" is raised to the negative power so it has to move down.

(Note: The exponent of 3 here is 1. 3 does not have a negative exponent so it stays in its original place!!)

$$= \frac{3 \cdot 1}{x^4} = \frac{3}{x^4}$$

Example: $-5m^{-8}n^2/x^{10}y^{-5}$

Solution: $-5y^5n^2/m^8x^{10}$ (Variables "y" and "m" have been moved with their negative powers to make them positive powers, "n" and "x" don't move since they have positive powers.)

Example: $12^{-4}(12^8)$

Solution: Using negative power rule, move 12^{-4} to the denominator and make it positive exponent $12^4 = \dfrac{1 \cdot 12^8}{12^4}$ (negative power rule)

$= 12^{8-4} = 12^4$ (quotient rule, subtract powers)

147.   **How do you simplify an expression when more than one of the exponent rules are combined into one problem?**

Try to follow a certain order. Here is one method:

- **D**istribute powers to all, including coefficients
- **E**valuate number coefficient terms
- **R**educe coefficient terms
- **M**ove negatives
- **A**dd exponents of same side like variables
- **S**ubtract exponents of divided like variables

DERMAS: Multiply to distribute powers outside parenthesis, **Evaluate** coefficients, **Reduce** coefficients, **Move** negative exponent variables, **Add** like variable powers, **Subtract** like variable power

Example: $(5a^4b^6)(12abc)^0(-2a^2bc^5)$

Solution: Following the **DERMAS** sequence

$(5a^4b^6)(1)(-2a^2bc^5)$	(Zero power rule)
$=(5)(-2)a^{4+2}b^{6+1}c^5$	(Product rule, Add)
$=-10a^6b^7c^5$	(Final Answer)

Example: $\dfrac{-42m^6n^{-3}p^5}{6m^{11}n^{-5}p^5}$

Solution: Following the **DERMAS** sequence

$=\dfrac{-42m^6\,n^{-3}\,p^5}{6m^{11}n^{-5}p^5}$	(Given)
$=\dfrac{-7m^6\,n^5\,p^5}{m^{11}\,n^3\,p^5}$	(Move the negative exponent variables, reduce coefficients)
$=\dfrac{-7\,n^{5-3}\,p^{5-5}}{m^{11-6}}$	(Add/Subtract exponents, zero power rule)
$=\dfrac{-7\,n^2}{m^5}$	(Final Answer)

Example: $\dfrac{(-3ab^6)^5}{(-a^5b^2)^7}$

Solution: Following the **DERMAS** sequence

$=\dfrac{(-3)^5a^5b^{30}}{(-1)^7a^{35}b^{14}}$	(Power to power rule)
$=\dfrac{-243a^5b^{30}}{-1a^{35}b^{14}}$	(Reduce coefficients)
$=\dfrac{243b^{30-14}}{a^{35-5}}$	(Quotient rule)
$=\dfrac{243b^{16}}{a^{30}}$	(Final Answer)

Example: $\dfrac{2m^7n^3 \cdot (3mp^8)^3}{(3n^5p^{-3})^2 \, 2mn^6}$

Solution: Following the **DERMAS** sequence

$= \dfrac{2m^7n^3}{3^2n^{10}p^{-6}} \cdot \dfrac{3^3m^3p^{24}}{2mn^6}$	(Distribute powers power rule)
$= \dfrac{2m^7n^3}{9n^5p^{-6}} \cdot \dfrac{27m^3p^{24}}{2mn^6}$	(Evaluate exponents)
$= \dfrac{54m^7\,m^3n^3p^{24}}{18mn^{11}p^{-6}}$	(Multiply coefficients)
$= \dfrac{3m^{10}n^3p^{24}}{mn^{11}p^{-6}}$	(Reduce coefficients)
$= \dfrac{3m^{10}n^3p^{24}\,p^6}{mn^{11}}$	(Move negative powers)
$= \dfrac{3\,m^{7+3-1}p^{24+6}}{n^{11-3}}$	(Add and subtract powers of like variables)
$= \dfrac{3m^9p^{30}}{n^8}$	(Final Answer)

Example: $(7xy)(-x^4y^3)^5(2x^5y^6)^{-2}$

Solution: Following the **DERMAS** sequence

$= (7xy)(-1^5x^{20}y^{15})(2^{-2}x^{-10}y^{-12})$	(Distribute powers by Power rule) (Move the negative power terms to make them positive powers)
$= \dfrac{(7xy)(-1x^{20}y^{15})}{2^2\,x^{10}y^{12}}$	(Negative power rule)
$= -\dfrac{(7xy)(x^{20}y^{15})}{4.x^{10}y^{12}}$	(Simplify coefficients)
$= -\dfrac{7\,x^{1+20}\,y^{1+15}}{4\,x^{10}y^{12}}$	(Add exponents using product rule)
$= -\dfrac{7\,x^{21-10}\,y^{16-12}}{4}$	(Subtract exponents using quotient rule)
$= -\dfrac{7x^{11}y^4}{4}$	(Final answer)

Example: $(2)^{-5}$
Solution:

$\left(\frac{1}{2}\right)^5$	(Apply the negative power rule first)
$\frac{1^5}{2^5}$	(Power rule: Distribute powers)
$\left(\frac{1}{2} \cdot \frac{1}{2} \cdot \frac{1}{2} \cdot \frac{1}{2} \cdot \frac{1}{2}\right)$	(Expand)
$\frac{1}{32}$	(Multiply out the base to the exponent) (Final answer)

Example: $\left(\frac{5^8}{5^{-2}}\right) \div \left(\frac{5^{-6}}{5^7}\right)$

Solution:

$= 5^{8-(-2)} \div 5^{-6-7}$	(Quotient rule)
$= 5^{10} \div 5^{-13}$	(Quotient Rule) *(Note: We are not using the negative exponent rule. This is an alternate way of solving)*
$= 5^{10-(-13)}$	(Quotient rule)
$= 5^{23}$	

Example: $\left(\frac{x^{6m}}{x^{2m+3}}\right)^2 \left(\frac{x^4}{x^m}\right)^3$

Solution: Following the **DERMAS** sequence

$= \frac{x^{6m(2)}}{x^{(2m+3)(2)}} \cdot \frac{x^{4(3)}}{x^{m(3)}}$	(Power rule)
$= \frac{x^{12m}}{x^{4m+6}} \cdot \frac{x^{12}}{x^{3m}}$	(Distribute powers into parenthesis)
$= \frac{x^{12m+12}}{x^{4m+6+3m}} \quad = \frac{x^{12m+12}}{x^{7m+6}}$	(Product rule)
$= x^{12m + 12 - (7m + 6)} = x^{12m + 12 - 7m - 6}$	(Quotient rule)
$= x^{5m + 6}$	(Final Answer)

148.   What happens to the power when it is transposed or moved to the other side?

Reciprocal power rules states that powers can be moved from one side of the equation to the other by inverting the fraction and raising the term on the other side to the new exponent.

Reciprocal of exponent(Flip the exponent)

If $(x)^{m/n}$ = y then x = $(y)^{n/m}$

Example: $x^{3/2} = 8$
Solution: $x = 8^{2/3}$

Take the root first; 3rd root of 8 is 2.
Then apply the power, $x = 2^2 = 4$

---

149.   What is the square root of x to any exponent x^n?

To find the square root of x^n simple divide the exponent by 2 which gives $x^{n/2}$. If "n" is even "n/2" will be a whole number if "n" is odd "n/2" will be a fraction.
Example: Square root of $x^4 = x^{4/2} = x^2$
Solution: Square root of $x^3 = x^{3/2} = x\sqrt{x}$

---

150.   How do you take the nth root of x^m?

In general, to take any nth root divide the exponent "m" by "n", The nth root of $x^m = x^{m/n}$. If the exponent is not a whole number then divide m/n. You get two parts, a whole number quotient part and a remainder. Write the whole number quotient part outside and remainder part back in the radical. This is the irrational part
Example: Find the cube root of x^{11}
Solution: $x^{11/3}$

Dividing $11/3 = 3$; Remainder 2 yields $x^3 \sqrt[3]{x^2}$

(Quotient Part.Irrational Part)

---

151.   How do you solve fractional exponents?

The numerator is the power the number is raised to and the denominator is the radical.

$$x^{a/b} = \sqrt[b]{x^a}$$

(Numerator = Inside Power; Denominator = Outside Radical Index)
Example: $16^{3/2}$
Solution: This is equivalent to $(16^3)^{1/2}$

$$= \sqrt{16^3}$$
$$= 4^3$$
$$= 64$$

152.   **What is scientific notation?**

Scientific notation is when a number is written as a product of a decimal and power of 10. The decimal can only have one digit in front of it from 1-9. Scientific notation is used to convey order of magnitude.

Example: 4.035×10^3

---

153.   **How do you convert a number to scientific notation?**

To convert a number to scientific notation, move the decimal point so that there is only one number in front of the decimal point between 1 and 9. If you moved the decimal place to the left "n" places raise 10 to the number "n" or add "n" to the already existing exponent of 10. If you moved the decimal right "n" places then add a negative "n" exponent to 10 or subtract "n" from the exponent of 10.

Example: Convert 4203.5 to scientific notation

Solution: 4203.5 (The decimal point will be moved 3 places left)

4.2035×10^3 (This means we need to multiply by 10^3)

Example: Convert 0.00042035 to scientific notation

Solution: 0.00042035 (The decimal point will be moved 4 places right)

4.2035×10^{-4} (This means we need to multiply by 10^{-4})

---

154.   **How can you apply exponent rules to scientific notation?**

Exponent rules can be used to simplify scientific notation problems.

Example: $(4.5 \times 10^{-3})(40 \times 10^7)$

Solution:

$4.5 \times 40 = 180$	(First multiply the numbers together)
$10^{-3+7} = 10^4$	(Add exponents)
180×10^4	(Rewrite)
1.8×10^6	(Rewrite in scientific notation. We move the decimal point of 180 two places left so we add 2 to the exponent of 10)

Example: $(4 \times 10^{-3})/(2 \times 10^7)$

Solution:

$4/2 = 2$	(First reduce the numbers together)
$10^{-3-7} = 10^{-10}$	(Add/Subtract exponents)
$= 2 \times 10^{-10}$	(Final answer)

Chapter 8: Radicals

- What are we going to learn about radicals?

  - Simplifying radicals

  - Solving radical equations with one radical

  - Solving radical equations with two radicals

  - Extraneous solutions

155.   What is the radical of a number?

The radical of a number is an expression under a root. It could be a square root, cube root or any other root. The number on the root sign(radical sign) is the index(Inverse power) and the number under the sign is the radicand or the base.

Example: $\sqrt[5]{32}$

It can also be written as $32^{1/5}$

The index here is 5 and radicand is 32 so it's the 5th root of 32=2.

Example: $\sqrt[3]{216}$

The index here is 3 so it's the 3rd root of 216.

It can also be written as $216^{1/3}$=6

156.   How do you simplify radicals?

First, rewrite the numbers as a product of a perfect square and a non-perfect square. The perfect square goes out of the radical as its square root. The leftover part inside is the non-perfect square.

Example: $\sqrt{300}$ = $\sqrt{3(100)}$

Solution: $10\sqrt{3}$

157.   **How do you simplify radicals with variables?**

Example: Simplify $\sqrt[4]{256x^7}$

Solution: Separating the numbers and the variables

$$\sqrt[4]{256x^7} = \sqrt[4]{256}\sqrt[4]{x^7}$$

Solve each part separately

$\sqrt[4]{256} = 256^{1/4} = 4$ (Fourth root of 256 = 4)

$\sqrt[4]{x^7} = 7^{/4} = x^{4/4} \cdot x^{3/4} = x^1 \cdot x^{3/4} = x\sqrt[4]{x^3}$ (When there is a fractional exponent, divide. The whole number exponent goes outside the radical it's the rational part and the remainder exponent stays inside the radical as the irrational part.)

Final answer: $4x\sqrt[4]{x^3}$

---

158.   **How do you solve Radical Equations?**

To solve simple radical equations we try to cancel the radical exponent by raising both sides to the same exponent.

Example: $\sqrt[5]{x^3} = 1000$

Solution:

$x^{3/5} = 1000$ $(x^{3/5})^{5/3} = (1000)^{5/3}$	(Raise both sides to 5/3 to cancel the radical 3/5) (On the left side the exponents 3/5 and 5/3 cancel each other)
$x = 1000^{5/3}$	(When simplifying $1000^{5/3}$, Denominator of exponent is applied first then the numerator)
3rd root of 1000 is 10 $x = 10^5$ $x = 100,000$	 (Final Answer)

---

159.   **What is an extraneous solution?**

Radical equations are different from linear equations. When solving radical equations for "x" we can get one or more solutions based on the degree of the equation. The solutions have to be plugged back in to see if the original equation becomes a true statement. If the original equation is not true after plugging in a number, then the solution is extraneous.

160.   How do you solve radical equations(square root on one side)?

To solve radical equations we try to eliminate the fractional exponents by raising both sides to the same power. **(Note: Always check for extraneous solutions.)**

Example: Solve for "x": $\sqrt{3x+10}+8=x$
Solution:

$\sqrt{3x+10} = x-8$	(Isolate the Radical)
$3x+10 = (x-8)^2$	(Square both sides)
$3x+10 = x^2-16x+64$	(Distribute the right side)
$x^2-16x+64-3x-10=0$	(Bring all terms to one side. Make the other side zero)
$x^2-19x+54=0$	(Combine like terms to get a quadratic equation)
	(Solve the above equation using the quadratic formula)
$a=1, b=-19, c=54$	(Identify a, b, c)
$x = \dfrac{-(-19)\pm\sqrt{(-19)^2-4(1)(54)}}{2(1)}$	(Quadratic formula)
$\dfrac{-(-19)\pm\sqrt{361-216}}{2(1)}$	(Simplify)
x=15.52 or 3.48	(Final answer)

Plug the solutions back in to check the answers for extraneous solutions. 15.52 is a solution. 3.48 is an extraneous solution.
(Note: **ISDTQE: Isolate, Square, Distribute, Transpose to one side, Quadratic Formula, Extraneous check.)

161.   How do you solve Radical Equations?

To solve radical equations raise both sides to the same power first then solve.
Example:Solve for "x"

$$\sqrt{3x-5} = \sqrt{2x+4}$$

Solution:

$\sqrt{3x-5} = \sqrt{2x+4}$	(First Step: Isolate the Radical, here both sides have radicals)
$(\sqrt{3x-5})^2=(\sqrt{2x+4})^2$	(Now square both sides)
3x-5 = 2x+4	(Square cancels the square root)
3x-2x=4+5	(Bring all "x" terms to one side)
x=9	(Final answer)

Plug the answer back in to check for extraneous solutions. 9 is a valid solution since 3(9)-5=2(9)+4 is a true statement.

162.   How do you solve radical equations(with square roots on both sides with a number term)?

The trick here is to square both sides <u>twice</u> after isolating one radical part.

Example: $\sqrt{3x+4} - \sqrt{2x-4} = 2$

Solution:

$\sqrt{3x+4} = \sqrt{2x-4} + 2$	(Take one radical part to the right side first to isolate one radical)
$(\sqrt{3x+4})^2 = (\sqrt{2x-4} + 2)^2$	(Square both sides) (Right side simplification) $(\sqrt{2x-4} + 2)^2 = (\sqrt{2x-4} + 2) \cdot (\sqrt{2x-4} + 2)$
$3x+4 = (2x-4) + 4\sqrt{2x-4} + 4$	(Square cancels the square root on the left side, foil on right side)
$3x+4-4-2x+4 = 4\sqrt{2x-4}$ $(x+4)^2 = 16(2x-4)$ $x^2 +8x+16=32x-64$ $x^2 -24x+80=0$ $(x-4)(x-20) = 0$ $x-4=0, x-20=0$ **x=4, x=20**	(Isolate radical again) (Square both sides again) (Factored form) (Zero Product Property)

Check for extraneous solutions by plugging into original equation.

(i)   x=4

$\sqrt{3x+4} - \sqrt{2x-4}$

$\sqrt{3(4)+4} - \sqrt{2(4)-4}$

4-2

2=2 (True)

(ii)   x=20

$\sqrt{3x+4} - \sqrt{2x-4}$

$\sqrt{3(20)+4} - \sqrt{2(20)-4}$

8-6= 2(True)

163.   How do you solve radical equations(with square roots on both sides with a number term)?

The trick here is to apply exponents both sides <u>twice</u> after isolating one radical part.

Example: $V = 4s^3$, Solve for s.

Solution: $V = 4s^3$. Isolate $s^3 = V/4$. Take cube root on both sides

$$s = \sqrt[3]{V/4}$$

Chapter9: Polynomials and Factoring

- What are we going to learn about Factoring?
  - First Step GCF
  - Difference of Squares
  - Difference of Cubes
  - Sum of Cubes
  - Basic Trinomial
  - Trinomial with "a" value other than one use ac method
  - Four terms factoring by grouping
  - Fourth and second power "u" substitution
  - Higher powers polynomials are factored more than once
  - Five terms

164.   What is a factor?

Numbers have factors, for example factors of 12 are: 1, 2, 3, 4, 6, and 12
Numbers that divide into the given number evenly without a remainder are called factors. Similarly polynomials have factors that are lower degree polynomials that divide into them evenly.

Example:

Number Factors   Polynomial Factors

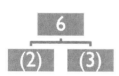   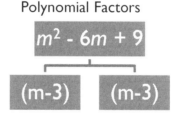

165.   What is the greatest common factor?

Greatest common factor commonly known as the GCF is the highest factor that is common to all the terms. For numbers, it is the greatest number that is a factor of all the terms. In other words it is the biggest number that divides all numbers evenly. For variables, it is the degree of x in all terms. Hence, it would be the lowest degree x term because it's the minimum power of the x's.

Example: Find the GCF of the polynomial $12x^3 + 16x^2 + 64x$.

Solution: GCF = 4x (4 is the greatest number, x is the lowest degree term)

166.   How do you factor a polynomial?

There are at least **10 types of factoring** problems. We need to identify which type it is to apply the correct method. The different factoring problem types are given below: Factoring means writing the polynomial as a product of two or more lower polynomials.

The different types of factoring problems are listed below. First step is to identify the type. Sometimes the type may not be visible until you factor out the GCF.

    a. **Polynomials with only Greatest Common Factor Method (Any number of terms)**

    b. **Two terms of the form $a^2 - b^2$ or Difference of Squares(Binomials)**

    c. **Two terms of the form $a^3 - b^3$ or Difference of Cubes (Binomials)**

    d. **Two terms of the form $a^3 + b^3$ or Sum of cubes (Binomials)**

    e. **Trinomials of the form x^2+bx+c by Sum and Product Factoring**

    f. **A polynomial of the form $ax^2 +bx +c$ with a number attached to x^2**

    g. **A polynomial of four terms**

    h. **A polynomial with two terms with a x^4 term**

    i. **A polynomial with three terms with a x^4 and an x^2 term**

    j. **Five term polynomial by three and two term method**

---

167.   **What is the first step in every factoring problem?**

The first step of every factoring problem is to factor out the **greatest common factor**. Then divide each term of the polynomial by this GCF. This will simplify the problem tremendously. If none, then continue with the methods explained below.

---

168.   **How do you factor using the Greatest Common Factor Method (Any number of terms)?**

Greatest common factor commonly known as the GCF is the factor that is common to all the terms. For numbers, it is the greatest number that is a factor of all the terms. For variables, it is the degree of "x" in all terms. So it would be the lowest degree "x"

Example: $32x^2 - 64x$

Solution: Factor Greatest common factor(GCF). For numbers, it is the greatest number that is a factor of all the terms. For variables, it is lowest degree "x". GCF=32x. Divide out each term by GCF

$$\frac{32x^2 - 64x}{32x \quad 32x} = x-2$$

Factor out the GCF and rewrite: 32x(x-2)
Can this be further factored by any other method? No.
Final Answer: **32x(x-2)**

169. **How do you factor two terms $a^2 - b^2$ using Difference of Squares Method (Binomials)?**

Factor out GCF first.

Then use, Difference of squares formula: $a^2 - b^2 = (a+b)(a-b)$

(square root of the first number+square root of the second number)times(square root of the first number-square root of the second number)

Example: $x^2 - 64$

Solution: Factor out GCF first. None here.

Difference of squares formula: $a^2 - b^2 = (a+b)(a-b)$

$x^2 - 64$

Square root of $x^2 = x$

Square root of 64 =8

Using the formula gives

$(x+8)(x-8)$

Can this be further factored by any other method? No.

Final Answer: $(x+8)(x-8)$

---

170. **How do you factor two terms $a^3 - b^3$ using Difference of Cubes Method (Binomials)?**

Factor out GCF first. Then use

Difference of cubes formula: $x^3 - y^3 = (x-y)(x^2+xy+y^2)$

Example: $x^3 - 243$

Solution: Factor out GCF first. None here.

Difference of cubes Formula: $x^3 - y^3 = (x-y)(x^2+xy+y^2)$

$x^3 - 243$

Cube root of $x^3 = x$

Cube root of 243 =7

Using the formula gives

$(x-7)(x^2+7x+7^2)$

Can this be further factored by any other method? No.

Final Answer: $(x-7)(x^2+7x+49)$

---

171. **How do you factor a polynomial of two terms $a^3 + b^3$ which are sum of cubes (Binomials)?**

Factor out GCF first.

Then use **Sum of cubes formula:** $x^3 + y^3 = (x+y)(x^2-xy+y^2)$

Example: $x^3 + 243$

Solution: Factor out GCF first. None here. Then use Sum of cubes formula.

$x^3 + y^3 = (x+y)(x^2-xy+y^2)$

$x^3 + 243 = (x+7)(x^2 - 7x + 7^2)$
Can this be further factored by any other method? No.
Final Answer: $(x+7)(x^2 - 7x + 49)$

---

172. How do you factor a polynomial Trinomials of the form ax²+bx+c.
Simple GCF then factor x²+bx+c using sum and product method. This means find factors that when added yield the middle term "b" and when multiplied yield the last term "c".
(x-/+Factor)(x-/+Factor). The signs depend on the problem.

Example: $3m^2 - 18m + 27$
Solution: Factor out GCF first.

$3(m^2 - 6m + 9)$
This is now a simple trinomial factoring problem. Find factors of "c" when added yield "b". Here c= 9 and b = -6 . -3 and -3 multiply to 9 and add to -6.
3(m-3)(m-3)
Can this be further factored by any other method? No.
Final Answer: 3(m-3)(m-3)

---

173. How do you factor a polynomial of four terms?
By Grouping Method

Group in sets of two. Factor out the GCF from each. Divide out the two sets of binomials by their GCFS. Final answer is (GCF1+GCF2)(Common Binomial)

Example: $8m^2 - 6m - 9m + 18$

Solution: Group in sets of two. First two terms are 8m²- 6m, GCF1 is 8m
Second two terms are -9m+18, GCF2 is -9. Now write these together.
8m(m-2)-9(m-2)
Remember, if the third term is negative to take out the negative GCF in the second group. Factors: (GCF1+GCF2)(Common Binomial)
Final answer: (8m-9)(m-2)

---

174. How do you factor a polynomial of the form ax² + b x +c with a coefficient of x² being other than 1?

For three term polynomials or trinomials with a number in front of x^2 use the "ac method"
(Note: ac method Hint (GMFR-GTGF))
Step1) Factor out **GCF(Greatest Common Factor) first**
Step2) **Multiply** "a" times "c"
Step3) Find **factors of "ac" that add to "b"**
Step4) **Replace the middle term** coefficient using new factors. Do not forget to write the variables with the new factors.
Now there are four terms so the next step is the **Grouping Method**

Step5) **Group in sets of two**

Step6) **Factor out GCF from each set divide out the terms**

Step7) **Final answer take the common term in parenthesis from both sets and write as the second factor and the outside GCFs added become the first factor.**

Example: $8x^2 + 10x - 3$
Solution:
- Factor out GCF first. Then use ac method.
- Multiply "a" times "c", then replaces b by factors of ac that add to b. Here ac=8(-3)=-24.
- List all factors of ac term -24. Start from 1 and go in order

Factor 1	Factor 2	Sum of factors
1	-24	1+-24=-23
-1	24	-1+24=23
2	-12	1+-12=-11
-2	12	-2+12=10
3	-8	-5
-3	8	5
4	-6	-2
-4	6	2

- Factors of 24 adding to middle term +10 would be -2, 12 Replace +10x by +12x -2x. Now it becomes a polynomial with terms and polynomial with four terms is factored by grouping.
- Group the first two together. Factor out GCF.
- Group the next two together and factor out GCF.

  $8x^2 + 12x$-$2x - 3$

- GCF step
  4x(2x+3) -1(2x+3)

  Now write the final answer factoring out the binomial, using insides and outsides.
- Final Answer: (2x+3)(4x-1)

---

175. **How do you factor a polynomial with Two Terms containing a x^4 term?**

Factor repeatedly using difference of squares formula

Example: $x^4 - 625$

Solution: Factor out GCF first.
Then use difference of squares formula

$$a^2 - b^2 = (a+b)(a-b)$$

What is the square root of x^4. It is x^2.
To find square root of x to any degree divide the exponent by 2.

$x^4 - 625$

$(x^2+25)(x^2-25)$. Further factor the difference of squares. Sum of squares cannot be factored.

Final answer: $(x^2+25)(x+5)(x-5)$

---

176.   **How do you factor a polynomial with three terms of the form**

ax^4+bx^2+c containing x^4 and x^2 terms.

Step1) To factor a polynomial with three terms with a x^4 and an x^2 term substitute y $= x^2$.
Step 2)Factor the quadratic.
Step 3)Replace the factors back as $y=x^2$. You will get two factors in x^2.
Step 4) Check for further factoring.

Example: x^4+4x^2+3

Solution: Factor out GCF first.

When you have a x^4 and a x^2 term substitute with y $= x^2$

The new simplified problem in terms of y is y^2+4y+3.
Factoring the simple trinomial gives

$y^2+4y+3 = (y+3)(y+1)$

Now replace y by x^2 since that was the substitution made earlier.
Check to see if this can be further factored.

Final answer: $(x^2+3)(x^2+1)$

---

177.   **How do you factor a polynomial with five terms using the three and two term method?**

To factor a polynomial with three and two terms method, factor the first three terms followed by the last two terms. The common factors of both groups factored out, gives the final answer.

Example: $x^3+4x^2+3x +2xy+2y$

Solution: Factor out GCF first.

Factoring three terms first: $x^3+4x^2+3x=x(x+3)(x+1)$
Factoring two terms next: $2xy+2y=2y(x+1)$

x(x+3)(x+1)+ 2y(x+1)
Factor out GCF (x+1) from the above two groups
(x+1)(x(x+3)+2y)= (x+1)(x²+3x+2y)
Check to see if this can be further factored.
Final answer: (x+1)(x²+3x+2y)

178.   What is a perfect square trinomial?

A perfect square trinomial is of the type $(a)^2 +(2ab) + (b)^2$. The advantage to look for these type of special polynomials is that they are very easy to factor to $(a+b)^2$. To check for perfect square trinomials, check if the first and last terms are squares. Middle term has to be 2 times the product of square roots of the first and last terms or 2.a.b. Similar with the negative also $(a)^2 -(2ab) + (b)^2 = (a-b)^2$

Example: Is $4x^2 +24xy + 36y^2$ a perfect square?

Solution: Here x=2a, y=6b. These are the square roots of the first and last terms.
The given trinomial can be rewritten as this
$(2x)^2 +2(2x)(6y)+(6y)^2$. First and last terms are perfect squares and middle term is in fact twice the square root of the first term times the square root of the second term so it can be factored as $(2x+6y)^2$

179.   What is the zero factor property?

If the product of two expressions A. B = 0 only one of those needs to be zero. Both factors can be zero but both "A" and "B" are not always zero, only one of them needs to be zero. Or/And is the keyword here.

Example: Solve (3x+4)(5x+4) = 0

Solution: Solve each factor separately 3x+4=0 or 5x+4=0 and the final answer is written as x = -4/3 OR x=-4/5

180.   How do you solve a polynomial by factoring?

To solve a polynomial by factoring,
First factor the polynomial. This step gives factors like
(x-solution1)(x-solution2)(x-solution3) etc. depending on the degree
Second apply the zero product property. Set each factor equal to zero and find x.

Example: Factor and solve $x^3-4x^2-4x+16=0$

Solution: Degree of the polynomial is three so we will get three solutions.
Since it is a quartic polynomial with four terms we use the grouping method. Solve means find the "x" values that make the equation true. So after factoring we set the factors equal to 0 and solve.
First take out the GCF from first two terms which is x^2 and GCF from the second two terms which is -4
x^2(x-4)-4(x-4)=0.
The factors are $(x^2-4)(x-4)$.
This can be further factored to (x-2)(x+2)(x-4)=0.
Now apply the zero factor property

x-2=0 => x=2
x+2=0 => x=-2
x-4=0 => x=4
Final answer x=2, -2 or 4

---

181.   What are like terms?

Terms with the same exact variables raised to the same exponent/power. Coefficients can be different.
Example: $20x^2$ and $5x^2$

---

182.   How do you add/subtract two polynomials?

When adding like terms, add/subtract the coefficients of the like terms and <u>do not change the powers</u>. Like terms have the same variables and powers so bring the like terms together and combine them into one term. You may have to add or subtract coefficients based on integer addition rules.
Example: Add $(20x^2 - 4x + 15) + (5x^2 + 2x - 10)$
Solution: Bring the like terms together and combine them into one term.
$= (20+5) x^2 +(-4+2)x +(15-10)$
$= 25x^2 +6x+5$

Example: $(16x^3 + 10x^2 - 4x +15) - (12x^3 + 13x^2 - 5x+2)$
Solution: Distribute the negative sign into the second equation. Then combine like terms.
$=16x^3 + 10x^2 - 4x +15 - 12x^3 - 13x^2 + 5x-2$
$=4x^3 -3x^2 +x +13$

---

183.   How do you multiply polynomials?

To multiply polynomials distribute all the terms in the first polynomial into all the terms in the second polynomial. To do this, **multiply the coefficients and add the exponents** from each term in the first polynomial to each term in the second polynomial and then combine like terms.
Example: $10x^2(2x^3 - 4x^2 +5x + 10)$. Multiply Polynomial by a monomial
Solution: Multiply coefficients and add exponents

$= 10x^2(2x^3 - 4x^2 +5x + 10)$
$\Rightarrow (10.2)x^{3+2} -(10.4)x^{2+2} +(10.5)x^{2+1} +(10.10)x^{2+0}$
$\Rightarrow 20x^5 -40x^4 +50x^3 +100x^2$

Example: $(3x-2)(3x+5)$. Multiply a Binomial by another Binomial
Solution: Distribute each term from first parenthesis into the second parenthesis. Remember to follow the rules of multiplication. Multiply the coefficients and add the exponents.

⇨ $(3x-2)(3x+5) = 9x^2+15x-6x-10$
Now combine like terms $= 9x^2+9x-10$

Example: $(5x + 3)(4x^2 + 10x – 2)$. Multiply a Binomial by a polynomial
Solution: Distribute each term from first parenthesis into the second
parenthesis.   Follow the rules of multiplication.
Multiply the coefficients and add the exponents for each term.
⇨ $(5x + 3)(4x^2 + 10x – 2)=20x^3+50x^2-10x+12x^2+30x-6$
Combining like terms, $20x^3+62x^2+20x-6$

Another method is the box method. Multiply each row with each column then add like terms.

Multipliers	$4x^2$	$+10x$	-2
$5x$	$20x^3$	$50x^2$	$-10x$
$+3$	$12x^2$	$+30x$	-6

Combining like terms after multiplying
$20x^3+50x^2-10x+12x^2+30x-6 = 20x^3+62x^2+20x-6$

184. How do you square a binomial?

A binomial is squared using the same rules as multiplying polynomials.
Distribute each term from the first parenthesis into each term of the second parenthesis.
Then, multiply coefficients and add exponents during each multiplication.
Example: $(3x+5)^2 = (3x+5)(3x+5)$
Solution: Use double distribution or FOIL
(First x First, outside x outside, inner x inner, last x last)
$(3x+5)(3x+5) - (3x)(3x) + (3x)(5)+(5)(3x)+(5)(5)$
$=9x^2+15x+15x+25$
$=9x^2+30x+25$

185. Is there a formula to square Binomials?

$(a+b)^2 = (a)^2 + (b)^2 +(2ab)$
$(a-b)^2 = (a)^2 + (b)^2 –(2ab)$
Example: $(3x+5y)^2$
Solution: Use the formula $(a+b)^2 = (a)^2 + (b)^2 +(2ab)$
Here a=3x, b=5y
$(3x)^2+(5y)^2+(2.3x.5y) = 9x^2+25y^2+30xy$
(Note: **Most common mistake: $(a+b)^2 = (a)^2 + (b)^2$. Look above for the correct formula)

186.   **How do you _simplify_ polynomial expressions(fractions) that contain the multiplication operation?**

Example: Simplify $\dfrac{x^2 - 5x - 6}{x^2 + 2x - 35} \bullet \dfrac{x^2 + 4x - 21}{x^2 - 9x + 18}$

Solution: 1) First factor each term separately.

$x^2 - 5x - 6 = (x-6)(x+1)$
$x^2 + 4x - 21 = (x+7)(x-3)$
$x^2 + 2x - 35 = (x+7)(x-5)$
$x^2 - 9x + 18 = (x-6)(x-3)$

2) Cancel or reduce terms

$$\dfrac{(x-6)(x+1)}{(x+7)(x-5)} \bullet \dfrac{(x+7)(x-3)}{(x-6)(x-3)}$$

(Note: ** Common Mistake "x" cannot be canceled when it is part of a group of terms or expression or polynomial)

Final Answer = $\dfrac{(x+1)}{(x-5)}$ (Remaining terms after canceling like terms)

---

187.   **How do you _simplify_ polynomial expressions(fractions) containing division?**

Flip the second fraction, Factor and Reduce

Example: Simplify $\dfrac{x^2 + 2x - 8}{x^2 + 2x - 35} \div \dfrac{x^2 + 5x + 4}{x^2 + 3x + 2}$

Solution: _(Note: You cannot cancel x^2 part of terms because they are part of polynomials)_
1) First convert the division to a multiplication operation by inverting the second fraction.

$$\dfrac{x^2 + 2x - 8}{x^2 + 2x - 35} \bullet \dfrac{x^2 + 3x + 2}{x^2 + 5x + 4}$$

Now factor each term
$x^2 + 2x - 8 = (x+4)(x-2)$
$x^2 + 2x - 35 = (x+7)(x-5)$
$x^2 + 3x + 2 = (x+2)(x+1)$
$x^2 + 5x + 4 = (x+4)(x+1)$

2) Cancel or reduce terms

$$\dfrac{(x+4)(x-2)}{(x+7)(x-5)} \bullet \dfrac{(x+2)(x+1)}{(x+4)(x+1)}$$

Final Answer = $\dfrac{(x-2)(x+2)}{(x+7)(x-5)}$ (Remaining terms after canceling like terms)

188.   **How do you reduce a polynomial expression to lowest terms?**

Example: Reduce $\dfrac{6x^2 + 25x + 14}{9x + 6}$

Solution: Factor $\dfrac{(3x + 2)(2x + 7)}{3(3x + 2)}$

Cancel common factors: $\dfrac{\cancel{(3x + 2)}(2x + 7)}{3\cancel{(3x + 2)}}$

Final answer: $\dfrac{(2x + 7)}{3}$

---

189.   **How do you reduce a polynomial expression to lowest terms?**

Example: Reduce $\dfrac{x^3 + y^3}{x + y}$

(Common mistake is to start canceling x and y with numerator)

Solution: Factor $\dfrac{(x + y)(x^2 - xy + y^2)}{(x + y)}$

Cancel common terms: $\dfrac{\cancel{(x + y)}(x^2 - xy + y^2)}{\cancel{(x + y)}}$

Final answer: $(x^2 - xy + y^2)$

Summarizing the formulas in this chapter:

$(a+b)^2 = (a)^2 + (b)^2 + (2ab)$
$(a-b)^2 = (a)^2 + (b)^2 - (2ab)$
$x^3 - y^3 = (x-y)(x^2+xy+y^2)$
$x^3 + y^3 = (x+y)(x^2-xy+y^2)$
$a^2 - b^2 = (a+b)(a-b)$

Picture: Factoring Polynomials Chart

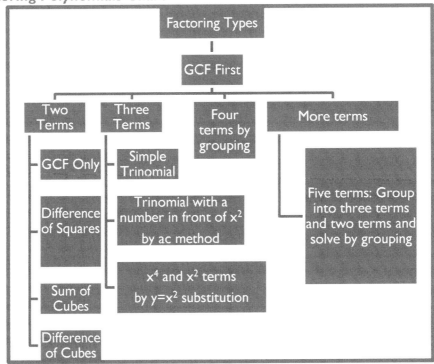

Chapter 10: Quadratics

- What are we going to learn about Quadratics?
    - Polynomial Degree
    - Roots to Equation
    - Equation to Roots
    - Quadratic Formula
    - Discriminant and Type of Roots
    - Factoring and Solve

190. **What is a quadratic equation?**

An equation with a highest degree of 2 is a quadratic equation. The general form of a quadratic equation is $ax^2 + bx + c = 0$. A quadratic equation has two solutions.

Example: $6x^2 + 7x + 8 = 0$ has a degree of 2 and has 2 solutions

191. **How do you solve a quadratic equation using quadratic formula?**

The Quadratic Formula can be used to solve equations that contain an x^2 term.

$ax^2 + bx + c = 0$

Solving means finding values for x that makes the equation true. Quadratic equations always have two solutions. Identify a, b, c from the equation and use the Quadratic Formula defined as

$$x = \frac{-(b) \pm \sqrt{(b)^2 - (4)(a)(c)}}{2(a)}$$

(Note: Learn the formula with parenthesis so you do not make mistakes with signs when simplifying)

Example: Solve $3x^2 -2x -5 = 0$ using quadratic formula.

Solution: Solve means find the value of x for which the expession is true.

First identify a, b, c

Here a =3, b=-2,c=-5 then substitute into the formula

$$x = \frac{-(b) \pm \sqrt{(b)^2 - (4)(a)(c)}}{2(a)}$$

$$x = \frac{-(2) \pm \sqrt{(-2)^2 - 4(3)(-5)}}{2(1)}$$

$$x = \frac{-(2) \pm \sqrt{64}}{2}$$

$$x = \frac{-2 \pm 8}{2}$$

Separate into + and -

x=(-2+8)/2   or x=(-2-8)/2

x=-5, x=3

192.   What are zeros or roots of an equation?

Zeros and Roots are the solutions of an equation. They are also the x-intercepts or where the graph crosses the x-axis. In the above example solving $3x^2 -2x -5 = 0$, -5, 3 are the roots of the given equation.

193.   How many roots does an equation have?

The number of roots(solutions) equals the degree of the equation.
Example: $3x^2 -2x -5$ has a degree 2 so it will have 2 solutions
$4x^3 -2x^2 -5$ has a degree 3 so it will have 3 solutions

194.   Given the roots of an equation how do you find the factors?
(x-Root1)(x-Root2)...

Example: Given 5 and 6 are solutions of an equation, find the factors
Solution: The factors are (x-5)(x-6)
(Note: Roots and factors are opposite signs)

195.   Given the roots of a quadratic equation how do you find the equation?
(x-Root1)(x-Root2)....=0

Example: If 5 and 6 are roots of an equation, find the equation.
Solution: If the factors are (x-5)(x-6) which when multiplied turns out to be
$x^2 - 11x + 30 = 0$

196.   What is the easy way to find the sum of roots of a quadratic equation $ax^2 + bx + c = 0$

The easy way to find sum of roots is by using the formula, Sum of roots = -b/a

197.   What is the easy way to find the product of roots of a quadratic equation $ax^2 + bx + c = 0$

The easy way to find product of roots is by using the formula, Product of roots = c/a

198.   Given the sum and product of roots of an equation how do you write the quadratic equation?

Use this equation to find the equation of a quadratic given the roots
$x^2 - \text{(sum of roots)}x + \text{(product of roots)} = 0$
Example: If 5 and -6 are roots of an equation, find the equation.
$x^2 - (5+-6)x + (5.-6) = 0$
$x^2 + x - 30 = 0$

199.   How many types of solutions are there?

There are two types of solutions: Real and Imaginary. Real solutions may further be categorized as rational and irrational.

200.   How can you tell the different types of roots without solving?

The discriminant defined by the formula "$b^2 - 4ac$" can be used to determine the types of roots or solutions.

201.   What is the discriminant?

The discriminant is defined by the formula $b^2 - 4ac$. It is the term under the radical in

the quadratic formula. $x = \dfrac{-(b) \pm \sqrt{(b)^2 - (4)(a)(c)}}{2(a)}$

202.   What is the discriminant used for?

The discriminant defined by the formula "$b^2 - 4ac$" can be used to determine the types of roots or solutions of a quadratic equation.

- If $b^2 - 4ac > 0$, the equation has two different real roots.
    - If the value is a positive perfect square, the equation has two different, real roots.
    - If the value is a positive non square number, the equation has two real, irrational roots
- If $b^2 - 4ac = 0$, the equation has two repeated real rational roots.
- If $b^2 - 4ac < 0$, the equation has no real roots.

203.   If $b^2 - 4ac > 0$, what are the types of solutions?

If $b^2 - 4ac > 0$, then the equation will have two real roots.
Example: $x^2 + 5x + 6 = 0$
Solution:

a=1, b=5, c=6	(Identify a, b, c from the given equation)
$b^2 - 4ac = (5)2 - 4(1)(6)$	(Find the discriminant, $b^2 - 4ac$)
$b^2 - 4ac = 25-24 = 1$	($b^2 - 4ac > 0$, So the equation has two real solutions.)
(x+2)(x+3)=0	(Factor)
x+2=0, x+3=0	(Solving using factoring and zero factor property)
x=-2, x=-3	(Two real roots)

204.   If $b^2 - 4ac = 0$, what are the type of solutions?

If $b^2 - 4ac = 0$, then the equation will have two real roots.

Example: If $x^2 + 6x + 9 = 0$
Solution:

a=1, b=6, c=9	(Identify a, b, c from the given equation)
$b^2 - 4ac = (6)^2 - 4(1)(9)$	(Find the discriminant, $b^2 - 4ac$)
$b^2 - 4ac = 36-36 = 0$	($b^2 - 4ac = 0$, So the equation has one real solution repeated)
(x+3)(x+3)	(Solving using factoring)
(x+3)(x+3)=0	(Zero factor property)
x+3=0, x+3=0	
x=-3, x=-3	(One real root repeated)

205.   If $b^2 - 4ac < 0$, what are the type of solutions?

If $b^2 - 4ac < 0$, then the equation will have no real roots.

Example: If $x^2 + 6x + 10 = 0$
Solution:

Here a=1, b=6, c=10	(Identify a, b, c from the given equation)
$b^2 - 4ac = (6)^2 - 4(1)(10)$	(Find the discriminant, $b^2 - 4ac$)
$b^2 - 4ac = 36-40 = -4$	($b^2 - 4ac = -4 < 0; \sqrt{-4}$ is an imaginary number. The equation has no real solutions.)

Since this value goes into the quadratic formula, this will make it a square root of a negative number, which is imaginary.

206.   Why is the discriminant $b^2 - 4ac$ so significant?

Because $b^2 - 4ac$ is part of the Quadratic formula which is used to solve equations. Since it ges under the radical, it makes it real or imaginary.

$$x = \frac{-(b) \pm \sqrt{(b)^2 - (4)(a)(c)}}{2(a)}$$

207.   **How do you solve a simple quadratic equation?**

Always isolate the square first. Then take the square root on both sides. Make sure you write plus or minus on the right side. (+/-) when you take square root of a number.

Example: $(x+3)^2 = 25$

Solution:

$\sqrt{(x+3)^2} = \sqrt{25}$	(Take square root on both sides)
$x+3 = +/- \ 5$	(Write +/- on the right side for the root)
$x = -3 +/- \ 5$	(Subtract 3)
$x = -3+5 = 3$	(Solve for x using the positive root)
$x = -3-5 = -8$	(Solve for x using the negative root)
$x = 3, -8$	(Final answer)

Example: $(x+3)^2 + 5 = 41$

Solution:

$(x+3)^2 = 36$	(Isolate the square first)
$\sqrt{(x+3)^2} = \sqrt{36}$	(Take square root on both sides)
$x+3 = +/- \ 6$	(Write +/- on the right side for the root)
$x = -3 +/- \ 6$	(Subtract 3)
$x = -3+6 = 3$	(Solve for x using the positive root)
$x = -3-6 = -9$	(Solve for x using the negative root)
$x = 3, x = -9$	(Final answer)

(Note: When taking square root of a number always write +/-)

Chapter 11: Quadratic equations and graphing parabolas

- What are we going to learn about quadratic equations and graphing parabolas?

    - Graphing quadratic equations

    - Vertex Form and Standard Form

    - Effect of a, h, k on the graph

    - Effect of a,b, c on the graph

    - Given three points find the equation of the parabola

    - Given vertex and a point find the equation of the parabola

208.   What does the graph of a quadratic equation look like?

The shape of the graph of a quadratic equation is a parabola or a U-shaped graph.

Picture40: Quadratic equation graph/parabola

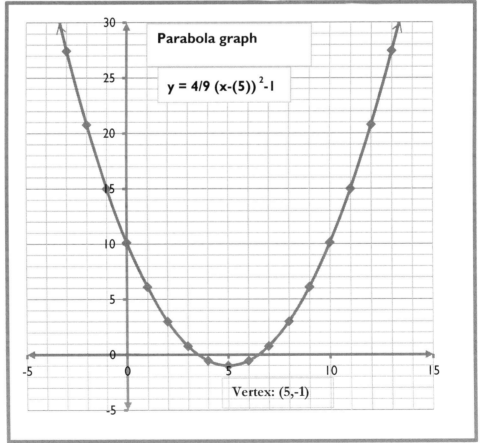

Parabola graph

$$y = 4/9 \ (x-(5))^2 - 1$$

Vertex: (5,-1)

209.   How do you graph a quadratic equation?

The graph of a quadratic equation looks like a parabola (U shaped). To graph a quadratic of the form $y = ax^2 + bx + c$ we look at the coefficients and constant a, b, c. To graph a parabola there are two methods: 1) **Table Method** 2) **Vertex and intercepts Method**

1) **Graphing using the Table Method: Make a Table, Plot.**

x	$y=x^2$ -6x-16
-2	0
-1	-9
0	-16
1	-21
2	-24
3	-25
4	-24
5	-21
6	-16
7	-9

2) **Graphing a quadratic equation using vertex, axis of symmetry, intercepts method**

The graph of a quadratic equation looks like a parabola or is U shaped. To graph a quadratic of the form $y = ax^2 + bx + c$ we look at the different numbers a, b, c. Find the vertex, axis of symmetry and intercepts

Step1) Find the vertex: Vertex Fomula x=-b/2a, y=f(-b/2a)

Step 2) Find the axis of symmetry: x=-b/2a

Step3) x-intercept: plug in y=0: solve the quadratic

Step 4) y-intercept: plug in x=0: solve for y

Step 5) Domain: $(-\infty,\infty)$, Range: Lowest, Highest

(Hint: VAI - Vertex, Axis, Intercepts)

Example: Graph: y= x^2 -6x- 16

a=1, b=-6, c=-16

Step1) Find the vertex: Vertex Fomula x=-b/2a, y=f(-b/2a)

Vertex x=-b/2(a) =-(-6)/2(1)=3. Plug in this number into the original equation to find "y" of the vertex.

y=f(-b/2a)=f(3)=$(3)^2$-6(3)-16=9-18-16=-25

Vertex (h,k)=(3, -25)

Step 2) Find the axis of symmetry: x=-b/2a

Axis of symmetry x=3

Step3) x-intercept: plug in y=0; solve the quadratic

0= x^2 -6x- 16

Solve by factoring or using the quadratic formula

0=(x-8)(x+2);

x=8 or x=-2

Intercepts: (8,0)(-2,0)

Step 4) y-intercept: plug in x=0: solve for y

$$y = (0)^2 - 6(0) - 16 = -16$$
$$y\text{-intercept} = (0, -16)$$
Step5) Domain: $(-\infty, \infty)$
Range: $[-25, \infty)$

Picture41: Parabolas $y = ax^2 + bx + c$

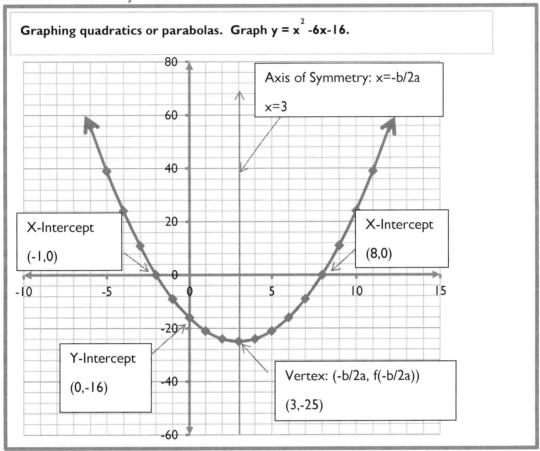

Graphing quadratics or parabolas. Graph $y = x^2 - 6x - 16$.

Axis of Symmetry: x=-b/2a

x=3

X-Intercept

(-1,0)

X-Intercept

(8,0)

Y-Intercept

(0,-16)

Vertex: (-b/2a, f(-b/2a))

(3,-25)

210.   What is the vertex?

Vertex of a parabola is the minimum or maximum point (depending on whether a is positive or negative respectively) at which the parabola turns.
Formula for vertex: x=-b/2a, y=f(-b/2a)

211.   What is the axis of symmetry?

Axis of symmetry is the line about which the parabola is symmetric. It passes through the vertex. It is found using the formula: x=-b/2a

212.   What do the numbers a, b, c, of the parabola $y = ax^2 + bx + c$ signify in graphing parabolas?

Value of |a|

- If |a| is greater than 1 for example 4, then the parabola is narrower. This is called vertical stretch.
- If the absolute value of a (|a|) is less than 1 for example ¼, then the parabola is wider. This is called vertical compression.

Sign of "a"

- If "a" is positive then the parabola is open upwards and has a minimum
- If "a" is negative then the parabola is open downwards and has a maximum value

Value of "c"

- The value of "c" is the y-intercept. If "c" increases, the parabola moves up. If "c" decreases, the parabola moves down.

Value of "b"

- The value of "b" is used in finding the vertex of the parabola which is given by (x = -b/2a, y = f(-b/2a))

213.   If the sign of "a" is negative, what is the effect on the parabola?

The equation of a parabola can be written as $y = ax^2 + bx + c$.

If the sign of "a" is negative the parabola is inverted. It is reflected on the x-axis.

Picture42: Parabolas- Effect of sign of "a" on a parabola $y = ax^2 + bx + c$

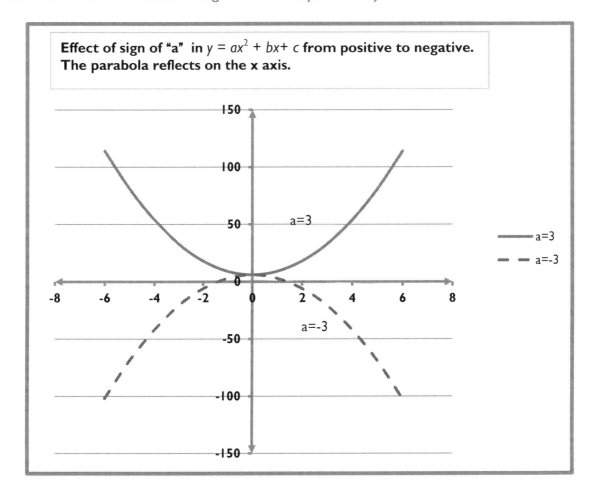

© Vaishali Patil

214.   If "a" value increases, what is the effect on the parabola?

The equation of a parabola can be written as $y = ax^2 + bx + c$.

If the absolute value of "a" increases the parabola stretches vertically.

Example: Comparing $y=3x^2+4$ with $y=7x^2+4$, the second equation is vertically stretched compared to the first.

---

215.   If the "a" value decreases, what is the effect on the parabola?

The equation of a parabola can be written as $y = ax^2 + bx + c$.

If the absolute value of "a" decreases, the parabola compresses vertically.

Example: Comparing $y=\underline{3}x^2+4x+6$ with $y=\underline{7}x^2+4x+6$, the second equation is more vertically stretched.

Picture43: Parabolas- Effect of "a" on a Parabola $y = ax^2 + bx + c$

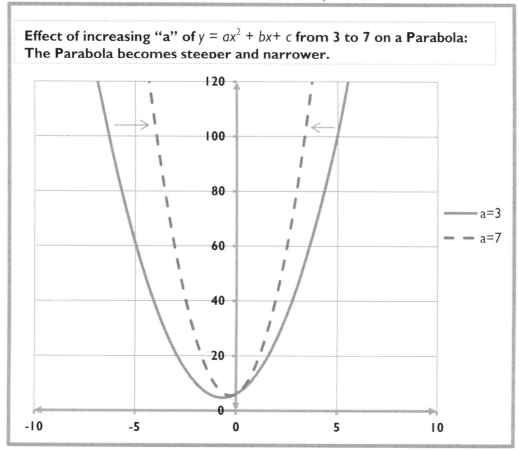

Effect of increasing "a" of $y = ax^2 + bx + c$ from 3 to 7 on a Parabola: The Parabola becomes steeper and narrower.

216.   If "c" value increases, what is the effect on the parabola?

The equation of a parabola can be written as $y = ax^2 + bx + c$.
If the absolute value of "c" increases the parabola shifts vertically up.

Example: Comparing $y = 3x^2 + 6$ with $y = 3x^2 + 18$, the second equation is vertically shifted up 12 units compared to the first.

217.   If "c" value decreases, what is the effect on the parabola?

The equation of a parabola can be written as $y = ax^2 + bx + c$.
If the absolute value of "c" decreases the parabola shifts vertically down.

Example: Comparing $y = 3x^2 + 4x + 18$ with $y = 3x^2 + 4x + 6$, the parabola is vertically shifted down 12 units.

Picture44: Parabolas- Effect of "c" on a Parabola $y = ax^2 + bx + c$

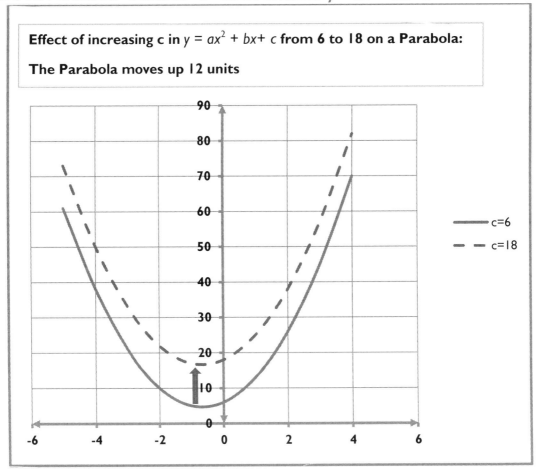

Effect of increasing c in $y = ax^2 + bx + c$ from 6 to 18 on a Parabola:

The Parabola moves up 12 units

218.   What is the equation of a parabola in the vertex from?

Equation of a parabola in vertex form is $y = a(x-h)^2+k$,

where (h,k) is the vertex of the parabola and value of "a" can be found by plugging in another given point on the parabola.

Example: Find the equation of the parabola in vertex form which has a vertex (3,4) and passes through (5,6)

Solution: Equation of a parabola in vertex form is $y = a(x-h)^2+k$

$y=a(x-3)^2+4$

Plug in point (5,6) for (x,y) to find the "a" value.

$6=a(5-3)^2+4$

Solve for "a"

$6=4a+4$

$a=1/2$

Final equation $y=1/2(x-3)^2+4$

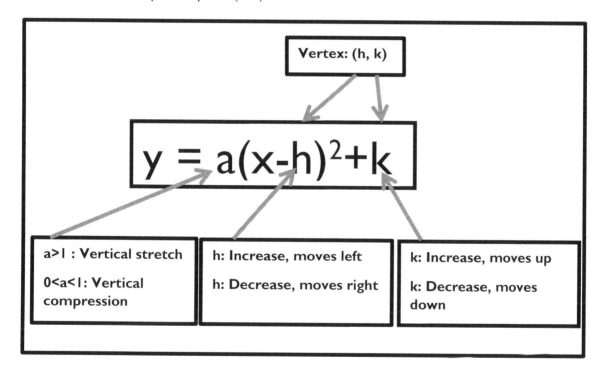

219. **What is the effect on the parabola if the "h" value is increased?**
Equation of a parabola in vertex form is $y = a(x-h)^2+k$
If |h| value is increased the parabola shifts to the right by number of units increased.
Example: If the equation changes from $y = 4/9(x-5)^2-1$ to
$y = 4/9(x-10)^2-1$ the parabola shifts right 5 places.

220. **What is the effect on the parabola if the "h" value is decreased?**
Equation of a parabola in vertex form is $y = a(x-h)^2+k$
If |h| value is decreased, the parabola shifts left by number of units decreased.

Picture45: Parabolas- Effect of h on a Parabola

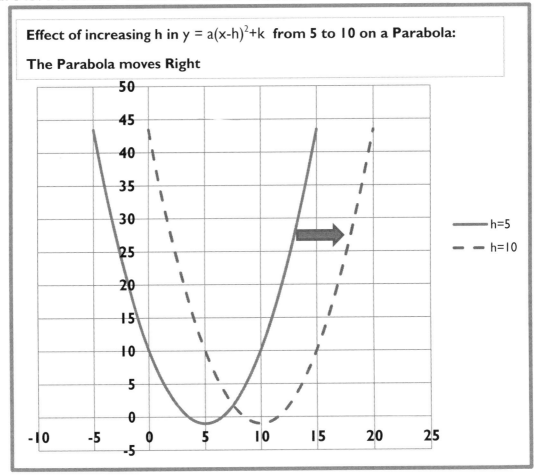

221.   What is the effect on the parabola if the "k" value is increased?
Equation of a parabola in vertex form is $y = a(x-h)^2 + k$

If the "k" value is increased the parabola shifts vertically up.

Example: If the equation changes from $y = 4/9(x-5)^2 - 1$ to $y = 4/9(x-5)^2 + 20$ the parabola shifts up 21 units.

222.   What is the effect on the parabola if the "k" value is decreased?
Equation of a parabola in vertex form is $y = a(x-h)^2 + k$

If the "k" value is decreased the parabola shifts vertically down.

Picture46: Parabolas- Effect of k on a Parabola

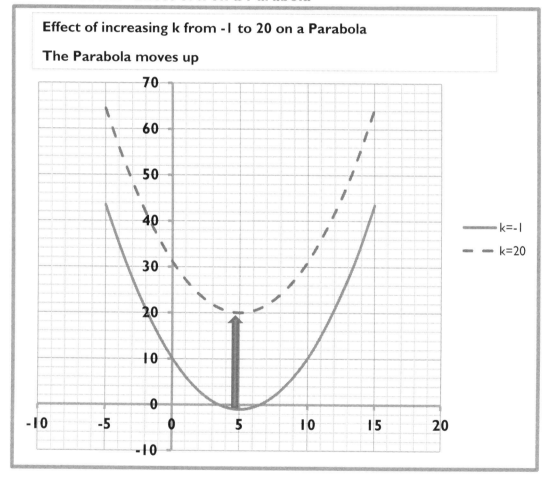

223.   **How do you change the equation of a parabola from the vertex form to the standard form?**

$y = a(x-h)^2+k$

Expand and combine like terms

$y = a(x^2-2xh+h^2)+k$

$y=ax^2-2axh+(ah^2+k)$ (This is of the form **$y = ax^2+bx+c$**)

Example: $y = 3(x-2)^2+6$

Solution: $y = 3(x^2-4x+4)+6$

$y=3x^2-12x+12+6$

$y=3x^2-12x+18$

---

224.   **How do you complete a square x^2+bx?**

Completing the square can be done by adding the term $(b/2)^2$

Example: Complete the square x^2+12x+_____

Solution: a=1, b=12, c=?

Add $(\frac{b}{2})^2 =(\frac{12}{2})^2=6^2=36$

$x^2+12x+36$

This is a perfect square $(x+6)^2$

(Note: If there is a number coefficient other than one for x^2 as in ax^2+bx, then you have to factor an "a" out from both terms before adding the third term.)

---

225.   **How do you change the equation of a parabola from the standard form ($y = ax^2+bx+c$) to vertex form ($y=a(x-h)^2+k$)?**

Step1) First find the vertex using the formula x=-b/2a; y = f(- b/2a)

Step 2) Write equation with the newly found h, k.

$y = a(x-h)^2+k$

(Note: this is completing the square method)

Example: $y=3x^2-12x+18$

Solution: Step1) Find the vertex (h,k) h=-b/2a = -(-12)/2(3) = 12/6=2

Plug in "h" into the original equation to find "k"

k= $3(2)^2-12(2)+18=12-24+18=6$

Equation: $y= a(x-2)^2+6$

Here a = 3 since the equation is $3x^2-12x+18$

$y= 3(x-2)^2+6$

(Note: When finding the vertex form from a graph, you may have to plug in a point picked from the graph to find "a" the coefficient of x^2)

226.   Given 3 points $(x_1,y_1)(x_2,y_2)(x_3,y_3)$ how do you find the equation of the parabola?

Given 3 points $(x_1,y_1)(x_2,y_2)(x_3,y_3)$ to find the equation of a parabola,

Step1) Use $y = ax^2+bx+c$ and plug in each point separately for (x, y)

$$y_1 = ax_1^2+bx_1+c$$
$$y_2 = ax_2^2+bx_2+c$$
$$y_3 = ax_3^2+bx_3+c$$

Now you have a system of three equations and 3 unknowns.

Step2) Solve the system to find a, b, c values and solve the equation.

Example: A parabola passes through (2,3) (0,1) and (-1,4). Find the equation.

Solution:
$$y_1 = ax_1^2+bx_1+c$$
$$y_2 = ax_2^2+bx_2+c$$
$$y_3 = ax_3^2+bx_3+c$$
$$3 = a(2)^2+b(2)+c$$
$$1 = a0^2+b0+c$$
$$4 = a(-1)^2+b(-1)+c$$
$$3 = 4a+2b+c$$
$$1 = c$$
$$4 = a-b+c$$

Using the above system, solve for a, b, c
$$c=1,$$
$$3=4a+2b+1$$
$$4=a+b+1$$
$$c=1$$
$$2=4a+2b$$
$$3=a+b$$

Solving the above system for a and b
$$2=4a+2b$$
$$-6=-2a-2b$$
$$-4=2a$$
$$a=-2, b=5, c=1$$

The final equation of the parabola is $y= -2x^2+5x+1$

---

227.   Given the vertex and one point how do you find the equation of a parabola?

Given the vertex and one point,

Step 1) Plug in the vertex (h,k) first and write the equation $y = a(x-h)^2 +k$

Step 2) Now the only unknown number is a.

Plug in the point given for "x" and "y" and solve for "a" value.

Example: Find the equation of a parabola passing through (2, 3) and has a vertex at (5, -1)

Solution: Step 1) Plug in the vertex (h,k) first and write the equation $y = a(x-h)^2 +k$

$y = a(x-h)^2 +k$

$y = a(x-(5))^2 -1$

Step 2) Now the only unknown number is a. Plug-in the point given for "x" and "y" and solve for "a" value.

$3 = a(2-5)^2 -1$

$4 = a(-3)^2$

$a = \frac{4}{9}$

Final answer: $y = \frac{4}{9}(x-(5))^2 -1$

Picture47: Parabola given vertex and a point

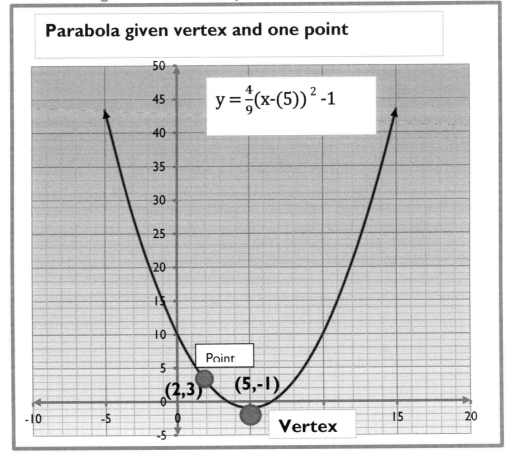

228.   How do you solve a quadratic by completing the square method?

As the name suggests we first make a perfect square and then solve by taking square roots.

Example: Solve $2x^2-5x-12=0$ by completing the square method

Solution: Step1) Move the constant to the right side

$$2x^2-5x-12 = 0$$
$$2x^2-5x=12$$

Step2) Take out coefficient of x^2, 2 here, as a common factor, divide the left side by 2. Write GCF outside the parenthesis.

$$2(x^2 - \frac{5}{2}x) = 12$$

Step3) Divide by 2 on both sides

$$(x^2 - \frac{5}{2}x+\underline{\quad}) = 6+\underline{\quad}$$

Step 4) Complete the square by adding a third term on both sides to complete the square. The third term to be added is $(\frac{b}{2})^2$

Here b= $-(\frac{5}{2})$ so $(\frac{b}{2})= -(\frac{5}{4})$ and $(\frac{b}{2})^2= (\frac{25}{16})$

$$(x^2 - \frac{5}{2}x+\frac{25}{16}) = 6 +(\frac{25}{16})$$

Step 5) Write the perfect square on the left side.

$$(x- \frac{b}{2})^2$$
$$(x- \frac{5}{4})^2 = \frac{121}{16}$$

Take the square root both sides

Step 6) When taking square root always write +/- for the number side.

$$x - \frac{5}{4}=+/- \sqrt{\frac{121}{16}}$$
$$x - \frac{5}{4}=+/- \frac{11}{4}$$
$$x=\frac{5}{4}+/- \frac{11}{4}$$
$$x=\frac{5}{4}+\frac{11}{4}=\frac{16}{4}, x= 4$$
$$x=\frac{5}{4} - \frac{11}{4}= -\frac{6}{4}, x=-\frac{3}{2}$$

229.   What is an Exponential Function?

An exponential function is a function where a number is raised to an expression with a variable in the power(such as "x"). General Equation of an exponential function:

$$y=a(b)^{x-h} +k$$

Vertical Stretch or Compression: compression 0<a<1, stretch a>1

Growth or Decay Factor b: growth b>1, decay b<1

Horizontal shift left for +h or x-h, right for –h or x+h

Vertical Shift k up for +k, down for –k

230.   **What is a growth function?**

Growth function is an exponential function where "y" increases exponentially as "x".
Growth function has a factor b>1

$$y = a(b)^{x-h} + k$$

Growth function example: $k(x) = 2(3)^{x-1} + 4$ (Since growth factor 3>1)

Example:

$$g(x) = 2\left(\frac{5}{3}\right)^x - 4$$

Picture48: Exponential Function Graph (Growth function)

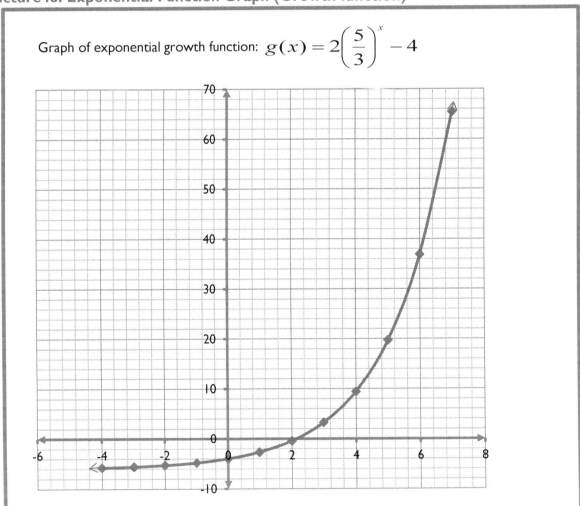

Graph of exponential growth function: $g(x) = 2\left(\frac{5}{3}\right)^x - 4$

231.   What is a decay function?

Decay function is an exponential function where where "y" decreases exponentially as "x". Decay function has a factor b< 1.

$$y = a(b)^{x-h} +k$$

Decay Function example: $h(x) = 2\left(\dfrac{1}{3}\right)^{x+1} + 10$ since decay factor 1/3 < 1

Picture49: Exponential Function Graph (Decay function)

Graph of exponential function: $g(x) = 2\left(\dfrac{1}{3}\right)^{x+1} + 10$

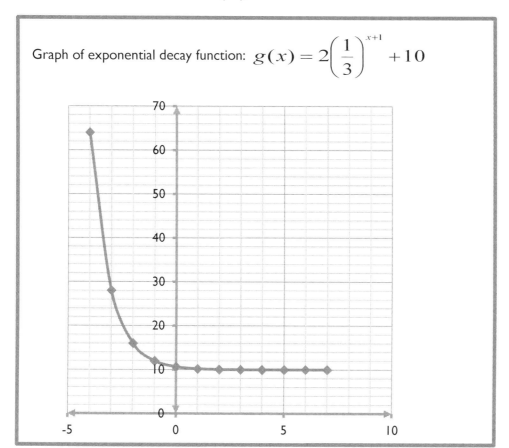

Graph of exponential decay function: $g(x) = 2\left(\dfrac{1}{3}\right)^{x+1} + 10$

© Vaishali Patil

232.   How do you find the equation of an exponential function?

An simple exponential function is of the form $f(x) = ab^x$. A transformed exponential function will be of the general form $f(x) = ab^{x-h} +k$ where "h" is the horizontal transformation and k is the vertical translation. We find the values of "a" and "b" from the given graph. Plug in the two points when x= 0, f(x)= 2. So 2 = a "b" is the slope value between x = 0 and x=1. And the slope between the x= 0 to x = 1 is 3. So b= 3. Plugging the The final equation is $f(x) = 2(3)^x$.

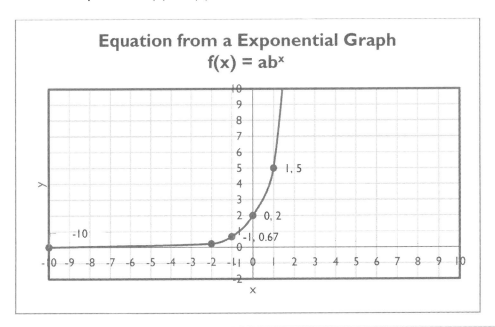

Equation from a Exponential Graph
$f(x) = ab^x$

More Special functions

233.   How do you graph

$$y = \sqrt{2x+3}$$

This is a square root function. The. The domain of this square root function is by solving the inside of the radical. Since negative numbers do not have square roots.

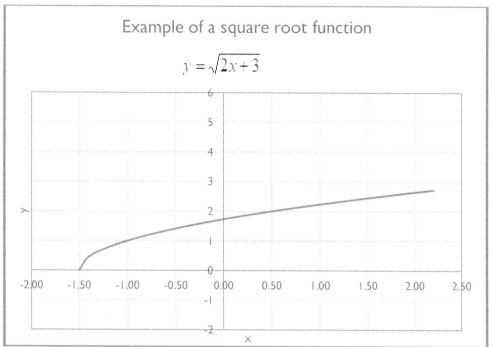

Example of a square root function

$$y = \sqrt{2x+3}$$

Important points
a) The domain of this function is x>= 3/2 you get this by solving the inside of the radical
"2x+3 >= 0" for x. Since negative numbers do not have square roots.
b) Range of function is y>=0
c) End behavior: $f(x) \to +\infty$ as $x \to +\infty$

234.   **How do you graph**

$$y = \sqrt[3]{x}$$

This is a cube root function. The. The domain of this square root function is by solving
the inside of the radical. Since negative numbers do not have square roots.

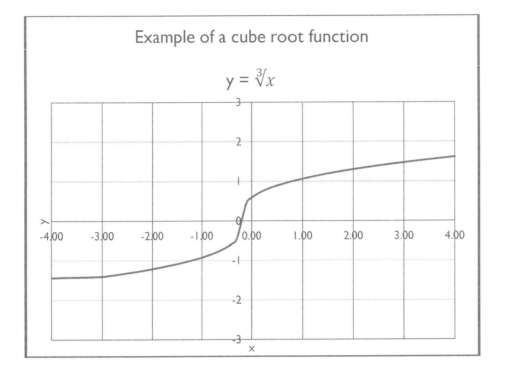

Important points

a) The domain of this function is $(-\infty, \infty)$

b) Range of function is $(-\infty, \infty)$

c) End behavior: $f(x) \to +\infty$ as $x \to +\infty$
$f(x) \to -\infty$ as $x \to -\infty$

---

235.   What is a rational equation?

A rational equation is one with a term that includes one or more terms with variables such as x in the denominator.

Examples: $\frac{1}{x} + \frac{1}{5} = \frac{4}{15}$; $\frac{1}{x+4} + \frac{1}{5} = \frac{4}{x+15}$

---

236.   How do you find the Least Common Multiple for polynomials?

Let's first revise what least common multiple means for numbers.

Example: LCM for numbers 40, 60 = 120. How did we find it?

Step 1) Write the prime factors of each term.

We first find the factors and then multiply the common factors and not common factors.

Factors of 40=<u>2.2</u>.2.<u>5</u>(Underlined numbers are common factors)

Factors of 60=<u>2.2</u>.3.<u>5</u>(Underlined numbers are common factors)

Common factors=<u>2.2.5</u>(Underlined numbers are common factors)

Not common factors=2.3

Step2) LCM: Common factors x Not common factors

(2.2.5).(2.3)=120

Example: LCM for monomials: $28x^3y^6z^9$, $120x^2y^4z^3$

Here we first find the LCM for the coefficients 28, 120

Step 1) Factors of $28x^3y^6z^9$ =<u>2.2</u>.7.<u>x.x.x</u>.<u>y.y.y.y</u>.y.y.<u>z.z.z</u>.z.z.z.z.z.z(Underlined numbers are common factors)

Factors of $120x^2y^4z^3$=<u>2.2</u>.2.3.5.<u>x.x</u>.<u>y.y.y.y</u>.<u>z.z.z</u>(Underlined numbers are common factors)

Step 2) LCM: Common times Not common factors

(<u>2.2. x.x. y.y.y.y. z.z.z</u>)(7.x.y.y.2.3.5.z.z.z.z.z.z)=$840x^3y^6z^9$

(Hint: For the variables use the highest power of each.)

Example: LCM for monomials and polynomials:

$4x^3$, x^2-3x-4, x(x-5), (x-3)

Step 1) Write out the prime factors of each term.

Factors of $4x^3$=<u>2.2</u>.x.x.x(Underlined numbers are common factors)

Factors of x^2-3x-4=(x-4)<u>(x+1)</u> (Underlined binomials are common factors)

Factors of 2x-10=2(x-5) (Underlined numbers are common factors)

Factors of (x-3)(x+1)=(x-3)<u>(x+1)</u> (Underlined binomials are common factors)

Common factors are <u>2</u>(x+1).

Step 2) LCM=Common x Not common factors=<u>2.2.(x+1)</u>x.x.x.(x-4)(x-5)(x-3)

= $4x^3$ (x-4)(x+1)(x-5)(x-3)

237.   How do you solve a rational equation?

To solve a simple rational equation find the LCM and multiply each term by the LCM. This reduces the equation to an equation without denominators. Solve the equation.

Example: Solve $\frac{1}{x} + \frac{1}{5} = \frac{4}{15}$

Solution:

$15x$	(LCM or common denominator of x, 5, 15 is $15x$)
$15x.(\frac{1}{x} + \frac{1}{5} = \frac{4}{15})$	(Multiply each term by 15x)
$15x.(\frac{1}{x}) + 15x.(\frac{1}{5}) = 15x.(\frac{4}{15})$	(Distribute 15x and cancel or reduce)
$15+3x=4x$	(Multiply)
$15=4x-3x$; $15=x$	(Final answer)

238.   How do you solve a rational equation with different denominators?

Example: Solve $\frac{x}{x-3} + \frac{x+3}{x-5} = \frac{18}{x-5}$

Solution: The LCM for the denominators: (x-3), (x-5), (x-5) = (x-3)(x-5)

One method is to multiply all the terms of the numerators by this LCM so denominators can be canceled.

$$(x-3)(x-5)\frac{x}{x-3}+(x-3)(x-5)\frac{x+3}{x-5}=(x-3)(x-5)\frac{18}{x-5}$$

After canceling factors we arrive at a quadratic equation

$(x-5)x+(x-3)(x+3)=18(x-3)$

$\Rightarrow x^2-5x+x^2-9=18x-54$

$\Rightarrow 2x^2-5x-18x-9+54=0$

$\Rightarrow 2x^2-23x+45=0$

Using the "ac" method factor

$\Rightarrow 2x^2-18x-5x+45=0$

$2x(x-9)-5(x-9)=0$ Grouping 2 terms by 2 terms

$(x-9)(2x-5)=0$

$x=9$, $x=5/2$. Check for extraneous solutions

$$\frac{9}{9-3}+\frac{9+3}{9-5}=\frac{18}{9-5}$$

$$\frac{9}{6}+\frac{12}{4}=\frac{18}{4}\ \text{True}$$

$$\frac{2.5}{2.5-3}+\frac{2.5+3}{2.5-5}=\frac{18}{2.5-5}$$

$$\frac{2.5}{-0.5}+\frac{5.5}{-2.5}=\frac{18}{-2.5}\ \text{True}$$

Final answer x= {2.5, 9}

---

239.   How do you simplify complex fractions?

Complex Fractions are considered as division of two fractions and hence flip and multiply the denominator fraction.

Example: $\dfrac{\frac{x-2}{3}}{\frac{x+3}{4}}$

Solution: $\dfrac{x-2}{3}\cdot\dfrac{4}{x+3}$

This is in prime factor form and none of the factors cancel out.

Final Answer: $\dfrac{4x-8}{3x+9}$

Chapter 12: Applications of Algebra

240.   **What are the keywords in converting word problems to algebra equations?**
- The keywords used for addition are: sum of, increased by, plus, more than, greater than, and total
- The keywords used for subtraction are: difference of, decreased by, minus, less than and lower than
- The keywords used for multiplication are: times, product, multiplied by and a factor of.
- The keywords used for division are: quotient, find each, divided by and ratio.

Consecutive integers problem

241.   **How do you solve consecutive integer problems?**
The keywords and variables used to solve consecutive integer problems are:
Consecutive Integers: x, x+1, x+2 …(since they differ by 1)
Consecutive Even Integers: x, x+2, x+4 …(Since they differ by 2)
Consecutive Odd Integers: x, x+2, x+4 …(Since they differ by 2)
Example: The sum of three consecutive even integers is 192. Find the integers.
Solution: Let first integer be = x
Then second consecutive integer = x + 2
And third consecutive integer = x + 4
Equation: x + (x + 2) + (x + 4) = 192
3x + 6 = 192
3x = 192-6
3x=186
x = 62
The integers are 62, 64, and 66.

Picture50: Consecutive even Integers

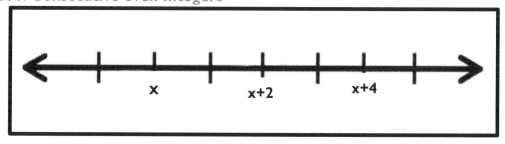

Coins Problem

242.   How do you solve different coin problems?

Aditya has a bag of 40 coins with a mixture of quarters and dimes totaling $6.25. How many of each coin is in the bag?

Solution: To solve coin problems we can setup a system of equations

No. of quarters=x; No. of dimes=y

First Equation: Number of coins equation: x+y=total coins

Second Equation: Value of coins equation:

(Value of type "x")times(#of coins "x")+ (value of type "y")times (#of coins "y") =total value

x+y=40

.25x+.10y=6.25

Using elimination method first solve for x from the first equation x=40-y

Plug the above into the second equation.

.25(40-y)+.10y=6.25

Distribute and solve

10-.25y+.10y=6.25

10-.15y=6.25

-.15y=6.25-10

-.15y=-3.75

y=25

Plug into original equation to find x

x+25=40

x=15

No. of quarters=15; No. of dimes=25

Distance problems

243.   How do you solve distance problems(toward each other)

Two cars start from a station and go in opposite directions. If the speed of the first car is 40 m/h and it takes them 4 hours to be 760 miles apart, find the speed of the second car.

Solution: Sum of distances=Total distance

$D_1+D_2=D$

Distance=Rate x Time

$r_1t_1+r_2t_2=D$

40(4)+x(4)=760

160+4x=760

4x=600

x=600/4

x=150

Speed of the second car=150 m/h

© Vaishali Patil

244. **How to you solve "distance" problems(same direction)?**

Train A leaves a station going due East at 50m/h. 2 hours later Train B leaves the same station going East. If Train B has a speed of 70 miles per hour how many hours will it take to catchup with train A. What is the distance travelled by Train A at this point?

Solution: Key here is the distance is the same.

$\qquad$ **Equation: Distance traveled by A = Distance traveled by B**

$\qquad$ **D1=D2**

$\qquad$ **Distance = RatexTime**

$\qquad$ $r_1t_1 = r_2t_2$

$\qquad$ 50t=70(t-2)

$\qquad$ 50t=70t-140

$\qquad$ 140=20t

$\qquad$ 7=t

Time = 7 hours.   Distance = Rate x Time=50(7)=350 miles

Breakeven Problems

245. **How do you solve "breakeven" problems?**

The revenue function of the swim supply store is given by R(c) =5c+10

The Cost function is given by C(c)=2c-5. Find the number of memberships "c" to be sold so that the company can break even or above which it can start making profits.

Solution: $\qquad$ **Breakeven: Revenue = Costs**

$\qquad$ **R(c) = C(c)**

$\qquad$ 5c+10=2c-5

$\qquad$ 3c=15

$\qquad$ c=5, 5 memberships have to be sold to breakeven.

Tickets Problem

246. **How do you solve "tickets" problems?**

The Lion King show tickets cost $40.00 for adults and $25 for children under 12. Last weekend, 100 more adult tickets were sold than children's tickets. The total revenue for that show was $13375.   How many adult tickets were sold?

Solution: Let the number of children's tickets = x; number of adult's tickets = 100 + x

Equation: $\qquad$ 12.50(x) + 20.00(100 + x) = 13375

$\qquad$ 12.50x + 2000 + 20.00x = 13375

$\qquad$ 32.50x + 2000 = 13375

$\qquad$ 32.50x = 11375

$\qquad$ x = 350

$\qquad$ # of children's tickets = x   = 350 tickets

$\qquad$ # of adult's tickets = 100 + x = 100 + 350 = 450 tickets

$\qquad$ There were 450 adult tickets sold for that Saturday show.

Ages Problem

247.   **How do you solve "ages" problems?**

The current ages of Amelia and Brown are in the ratio 1:3. Ten years from now, the ages will be in the ratio 3:5. Find the present ages of Amelia and Brown.

Solution: To solve for current ages lets setup the unknown variables for ages of

Amelia = x, Brown = 3x

After ten years,

Amelia's age = x + 10; Brown's age = 3x + 10

Given Ratio after ten years $\frac{x+10}{3x+10} = \frac{3}{5}$

By cross multiplying we get

5(x+10) = 3(3x+10)

Distributing on both the sides:

5x + 50 = 9x + 30

20=4x

5=x. This means Amelia is 5 years old and Brown is 15 years old.

Rectangle Problem

248.   **How do you solve "rectangle" problems?**

The length of a rectangle is 3 more than the width. If the perimeter is 18 find the length and width.

Solution: l=w+3

P=2l+2w

18=2l+2w

18=2(w+3)+2w

18=4w+6

12=4w

3=w; l=w+3=3+3=6

Length = 6, Width=3

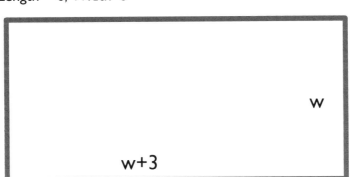

Perimeter = 18

w

w+3

Area Problem

249.   **How do you solve for the dimensions given the area of a rectangle?**
Example: Length of a rectangle is 2 more than its width. If the area is 48 square feet, find the dimensions of the rectangle
Solution: A=l.w
A=Area of the rectangle, l=length of the rectangle, w=width of the rectangle
l=w+2
A=l.w
48=(w+2)w
$w^2+2w-48=0$
(w+8)(w-6)=0
w=6, l=8 Length= 8 feet, Width = 6 feet

Investment problem

250.   **How do you solve "investment" problems?**
Michael invests $4000 in two accounts. The first account gives an annual interest of 10% while the second gives an annual rate of 6%. How much does he invest in each account if the total interest earned in one year is $280.
Solution: Let the investment in the 10% return account = x
The investment in the 6% account = 4000-x
Interest = PRT(Principal in $)(Rate in Decimals)x(Time in years)
Now make an equation for interest
%(Investment)+%(Investment)=Total Interest in one year
.10(x)+0.06(4000-x)=280
It is also easier to solve by moving each terms decimal two places to the right.
⇨   10x+6(4000-x)=28000
⇨   10x+24000-6x=28000
⇨   4x+24000=28000
⇨   4x=28000-24000
⇨   4x=4000
⇨   x=1000
So $1000 is invested in the 10% account and 3000 is invested in the 6% account.

Temperature Conversion Problem

251.   **How do you convert temperature from Celsius to Fahrenheit given the formula F=(9/5)C+32,**

Example: F=55°. Find C.

Solution. Plug in 55 for "F" value and solve for "C"

$$55=(9/5)C+32$$
$$55-32=(9/5)C$$
$$23=(9/5)C$$
$$23*5/9=C$$
$$115/9°= C$$

Upstream Downstream Problem

252.   **How do you solve an "upstream/downstream" rate problem?**

A boat can travel in a river upstream at 600 miles in 5 hours and the same distance downstream in 1 hour less time. Find the rate of the river and the rate of the boat in still water.

Solution: Distance=Rate.Time; Rate=Distance/Time

Let x: rate of the boat in still water

y: rate of the river

Downstream Rate: x+y= 600/4 (Given)

Upstream Rate: x-y=600/5 (Given)

$$\begin{cases} x+y=150 \\ x-y=120 \end{cases}$$

Solve the above system using addition method. 2x=270

x=135 miles/hr

Plugging x into the first original equation 135+y=150

y=15 miles/hr

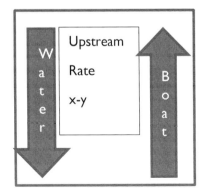
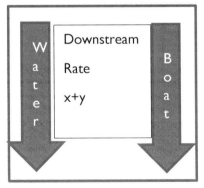

253.   **How do you solve an "upstream/downstream" rate problem?**

A boat can travel in a river upstream at 600 miles and the 800 miles downstream in the same amount of time. Find the rate of the river if the rate of the boat in still water is 80 miles per hour.

Solution: Distance=Rate.Time

Let x: rate of the boat in still water

y: rate of the river

Downstream rate: x+y

Upstream rate: x-y

Downstream time: 800/x+y

Upstream Rate: 600/x-y

Since the time is equal,

800/(100+y) =400/(100-y)

Cross multiply

800(100-y)=400(100+y)

8000-800y=4000+400y

12000=1200y

y=12000/1200 = 10

y=10 miles/hr

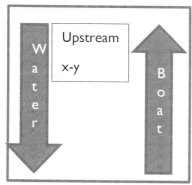 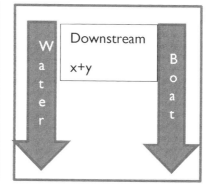

Work Problem

254.   **How do you solve "work" problems?**

Anita can finish painting a room in 20 hours. Alex and Anita can complete the same work together in 12 hours. How long does it take Alex to finish the painting job alone?

Solution: : $\dfrac{1}{Time\ taken\ by\ first\ person} + \dfrac{1}{Time\ taken\ by\ second\ person}\ldots = \dfrac{1}{Time\ taken\ together}$

Equation: $\dfrac{1}{x} + \dfrac{1}{20} = \dfrac{1}{12}$

LCM = 60x

$60x(\dfrac{1}{x} + \dfrac{1}{20} = \dfrac{1}{12})$ (Distribute the LCM 60x to each term)

6+3x=5x

6=2x

x=3

Alex takes 3 hours to finish the job of painting the room.

Mixture problem

255.   How do you solve "mixture" problems?

A chemist needs 600 ml of 20% Hydrochloric acid(HCl). He has 25% HCl and 12% HCl available. What is the volume of each he needs to mix to get the desired mixture?

Solution: Let the volume in ml of the 25% HCl be "x"

Then the volume of the 12% mixture is 600-x since we need 600 ml in total

Now make an equation

% available(Volume)+% available(Volume)=%(Total Volume needed)

$.25(x)+0.12(600-x)=.20(600)$

$25x+12(600-x)=12000$(It is also easier to solve by moving each terms decimal two places to the right.)

$25x+7200-12x=12000$

$13x+7200=12000$

$13x=12000-7200$

$13x=4800$

$x=4800/13=\$369.23$ ml of 25%

So $369.23 ml of 25%HCl and 230.77ml of the 12%HCl have to be mixed to get 600ml of the 20% mixture.

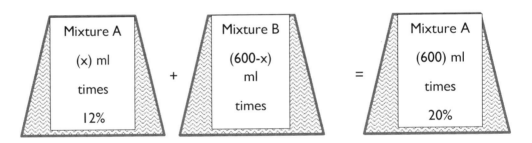

Garden with pathway Area Problem

256.   **How do you solve a "pathway" problem?**

A square garden with side "x" has a pathway built around it. The pathway has a width of 3 feet. What is the area of the garden? What is the area of the garden with the area of the pathway? What is the area of the pathway?

Solution: The area of the garden is A= side^2 or x^2. First find the side of the bigger square. Since 3 feet are added on both sides, the side length becomes x+2(3) =x+6. The dimensions of the bigger square which is the garden and the pathway are (x+6). So area of the bigger square is (x+6)^2. Drawing a picture always helps.

Area of the pathway= Area of (garden+pathway) – Area of garden
$$= (x+6)^2 - x^2 = (x^2 + 12x + 36) - x^2 = 12x + 36$$

Picture51: Garden with pathway Area Problem Picture

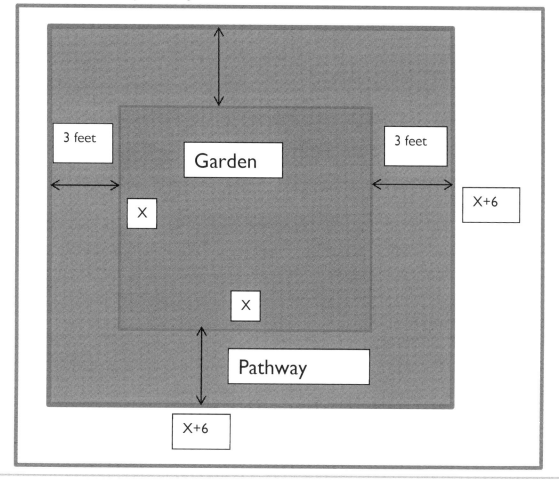

Vertical Motion Problems

Picture 52: Projectile motion graph

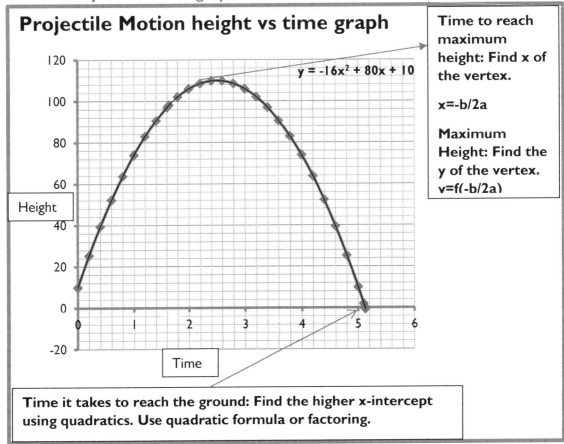

Projectile Motion height vs time graph

$y = -16x^2 + 80x + 10$

Height

Time

Time to reach maximum height: Find x of the vertex.

$x = -b/2a$

Maximum Height: Find the y of the vertex.
$v = f(-b/2a)$

Time it takes to reach the ground: Find the higher x-intercept using quadratics. Use quadratic formula or factoring.

257.   How do you find the height reached at a certain time?

$h = -16t^2 + v_0 t + h_0$

v_0 = the initial velocity in feet/second
h = the height in feet
h_0 = the initial height

Plug in the values for v_0, t, h_0 then solve for "h".

Example: Jason hits a tennis ball at the rate of 80 feet per second from a height of 10 feet above the ground. How high will it be after 2 seconds?

Solution: v_0 is the initial velocity in feet/second=80

h = the height at any time t=?
h_0 = the initial height=10 feet
t=2 seconds
Plugging all the given numbers into the vertical motion model we have
$h = -16t^2 + v_0 t + h_0$
$h = -16(2)^2 + 80(2) + 10$
$h = -64 + 160 + 10$ and h=106 feet. It will be 106 feet high above the ground after 2 seconds after it is thrown.

258. **How do you find the time it takes to reach the maximum height in vertical motion?**

$h=-16t^2+v_0t+h_0$

where v_0 is the initial velocity in feet/second

h = the height at any time t

h_0 = the initial height

Plug in the values v_0, h_0 then use vertex formula for finding the time to reach the maximum height. (x =-b/2a)

Example: A student hits a baseball at the rate of 80 feet per second from a height of 10 feet above the ground. At what time does it reach the maximum height?

Solution: v_0 is the initial velocity in feet/second=80 ft/s

         h = the height at any time t

         h_0 = the initial height=10

         t=?

         Plugging all the given numbers into the vertical motion model we have

                 $h=-16t^2+v_0t+h_0$

                 $h=-16(t)^2+80(t)+10$

         Here the x-coordinate is the variable "t" for time

         t=-b/2a = -(80)/2(-16)=-80/-32=2.5 seconds to reach max. height.

---

259. **How do you find the maximum height in vertical motion?**

$h=-16t^2+v_0t+h_0$

where v_0 is the initial velocity in feet/second

h = the height at any time t

h_0 = the initial height

Plug in the values v_0, h_0 then use vertex formula for finding the time to reach the maximum height. x =-b/2a, y=f(-b/2a)

Example: A student hits a ball at the rate of 80 feet per second from a height of
         10 feet above the ground. At what time does it reach the maximum height? What is the maximum height reached?

Solution:This problem is solved in two steps. The first step is similar to the previous problem.

Step1) First find the time it takes to reach maximum height then plug it in to find the maximum time reached.

         $h=-16t^2+v_0t+h_0$

         $h=-16(t)^2+80(t)+10$

         Here x is t

         t=-b/2a = -(80)/2(-16) =-80/-32=2.5 seconds

Step 2) To find maximum height, plug in the t value and find h. f(-b/2a)

         $h=-16t^2+v_0t+h_0$

         $h=-16(2.5)^2+80(2.5)+10$

         $h=-16(6.25)+80(2.5)+10$

         h=-100+200+10; h=110 feet (Maximum Height reached)

Projectile motion problem

260.   How do you solve a projectile motion problem?

A baseball is hit at the rate of 20 feet per second from a height of 10 feet above the ground. When does the ball touch the ground?

Solution: Find the x-intercepts

v_0 is the initial velocity in feet/second=20

h = the height =0 (Since it hits the ground h=0)

h_0 = the initial height=10

t=?

Plugging all the given numbers into the vertical motion model we have

$h=-16t^2+v_0t+h_0$

$0=-16(t)^2+20(t)+10$

$0=-16(t)^2+20(t)+10$

Solve using factoring or quadratic formula

$$t = \frac{-20\pm\sqrt{400-4(-16)(10)}}{2(-16)}$$

Simplifying the roots, the solutions are

t=1.63 seconds(Solution),   -0.38(extraneous)

Projectile Motion Equation
$h=-16t^2+v_0t+h_0$

h = the height at any time

t = time

v_0 = the initial velocity in feet/second

h_0 = the initial height

Summary of projectile motion concepts:

- To find time taken to reach maximum height: "x" of vertex x=-b/2a.
- To find the maximim height: "y" of Vertex y=f(=b/2a). Find –b/2a and plug into original equation.
- To find the time taken to reach the ground. Factor the quadratic or use quadratic formula to find x-intercepts. Choose the larger one.
- To find the height at a certain time, plug in the time for "t" and find "h".

Polynomials Geometry Problem

261. Find the area and perimeter of the triangle with polynomial sides.

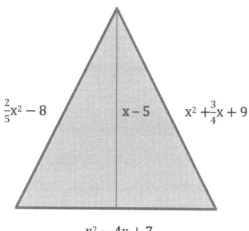

$$\frac{2}{5}x^2 - 8 \qquad x-5 \qquad x^2 + \frac{3}{4}x + 9$$

$$x^2 - 4x + 7$$

Solution:

a) Area of a Triangle = ½ base×height =1/2 $(x^2 - 4x + 7)(x\text{-}5)$

Using polynomial multiplication rules, 1/2 $(x^3\text{-}9x^2+27x\text{-}35)=\frac{1}{2}x^3\text{-}\frac{9}{2}x^2+\frac{27}{2}x\text{-}\frac{35}{2}$ square units

b) Perimeter of a triangle = Sum of all sides $=\frac{2}{5}x^2 - 8 + x^2 + \frac{3}{4}x + 9 + x^2 - 4x + 7$

$= 2\frac{2}{5}x^2 \text{-}3\frac{1}{4}x+8$ units

---

262. **Find the value of "x" given the angles of a triangle.**

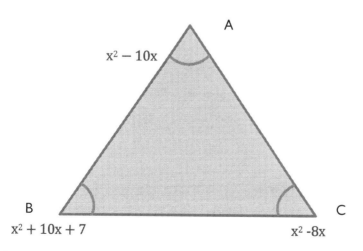

A

$x^2 - 10x$

B   C

$x^2 + 10x + 7$ x^2 -8x

Solution:

The sum total of the angles of a triangle =180°

$x^2 + 10x + 7 + x^2 - 10x + x^2 \text{-}8x = 180$

$x^2 \text{-}8x +180 = 0$

Factor and solve: $(x-18)(x+10)=0$; $x=18$

Similarity problem

263.   **Find the value of "x" given the following figure with similar triangles.**

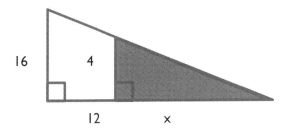

Solution: Since the two triangles are similar,

Height of larger triangle = Height of smaller triangle
Base of larger triangle   Base of smaller triangle

$\dfrac{16}{12+x} = \dfrac{4}{x}$ (Note: Base of larger triangle is 12+x)

Cross multiply and solve

$4(12+x)=16(x)$

$48+4x=16x$

$x=4$

Area Problem with polynomials

264.   **Find the area of the shaded region. All dimensions are given in feet.**

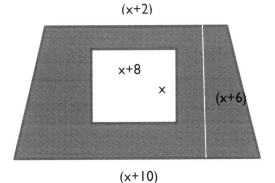

Area of the shaded region = Area of the trapezoid-Area of the small rectangle

Area of the trapezoid $=\frac{1}{2}$ (Base1+Base2)(Height)

$=\frac{1}{2}$ (x+2+x+10)(x+6)

$=\frac{1}{2}$ (2x+12)(x+6)

$=\frac{1}{2}$ (2x^2+12x+12x+72)

$=\frac{1}{2}$ (2x^2+24x+72)

$=$x^2+12x+36

Area of the small rectangle = BasexHeight

$=$(x+8)(x)

$$= x^2 + 8x$$
Area of shaded region = $(x^2 + 12x + 36) - (x^2 + 8x) = (4x + 36)$ sq ft.

Chapter 13: Absolute Value Equations and inequalities

- What are we going to learn about absolute value inequalities?
    - Solving and graphing absolute value equations a|bx+c|=d
    - Solving and graphing absolute value equations with less than inequality a|bx+c|<d
    - Solving and graphing absolute value equations with greater than inequality a|bx+c|>d

265.   **How do you solve an absolute value equation a|bx+c|=d?**
- First isolate the absolute value part.
- Separate the equation into two equations.
- Then solve for x from each.

The first equation is the same original without the absolute value symbols.
The second equation will have opposite signs on one side.

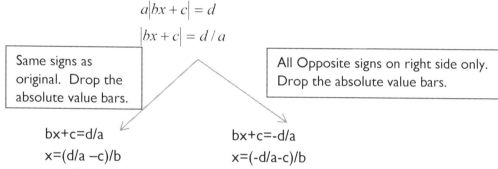

- Absolute value equations have two solutions. Check for extraneous solutions too.
  Typical solution has two numbers: {m, n}

Example: Solve   5|2x+3|=10

Solution: Divide by 5 to isolate the absolute value part

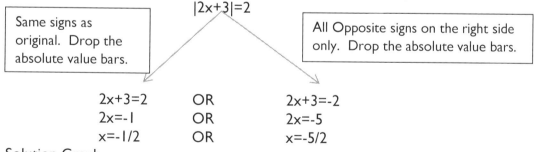

Solution Graph

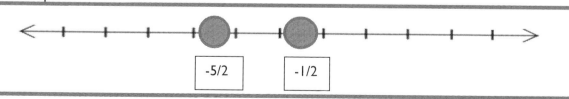

Final answer x={-1/2, -5/2}

266. **How do you solve an absolute value inequality with the less than and equal to relationship such as a|bx+c|≤d?**
- First isolate the absolute value part
- Separate the equation into two inequalities. The two inequalities are combined by the word "AND" (Less than = "AND")
- Solve for x from each. Combine the ranges with "AND". "AND" means intersection or overlap of the two lines

The first equation is the same original without the absolute value symbols
The second equation will have opposite signs on the left side

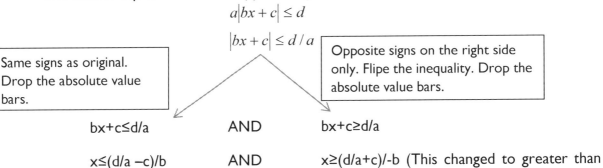

$$a|bx + c| \le d$$

$$|bx + c| \le d/a$$

Same signs as original. Drop the absolute value bars.

Opposite signs on the right side only. Flipe the inequality. Drop the absolute value bars.

bx+c≤d/a   AND   bx+c≥d/a

x≤(d/a −c)/b   AND   x≥(d/a+c)/-b (This changed to greater than due to division by a negative number)

- Graph on the number line
This will be a range of values on the number line.
- Write in interval notation. Typical solution is a range between two numbers: [m,n]
Hint: ISKSGI: Isolate, Separate, Keyword, Solve, Graph, Interval
Example: Solve 3|2x-5|+6< 12
Solution: ISKSGI: Isolate, Separate, Keyword, Solve, Graph, Interval
Isolate the absolute value part using opposite operations

3|2x-5|<12-6
3|2x-5|<12-6
3|2x-5|<6
$|2x-5|<\frac{6}{3}$
|2x-5|<2

Separate 2x-5<2   AND   2x-5>-2
Solve both new equations

2x<7   AND   2x<3
x<3.5   AND   x<1.5

Graph

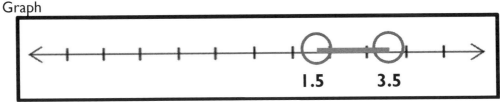

1.5   3.5

Interval Notation:(1.5, 3.5)

267. **How do you solve an absolute value inequality with greater than and equal to sign such as a|bx+c| ≥d?**

- First isolate the absolute value part
- Separate the equation into two inequalities. The two inequalites are combined by the word "OR". (Greater than = "OR") "OR" means the union or wherever the line passes through
  The first equation is the same original without the absolute value symbols
  The second equation will have opposite signs on the left side

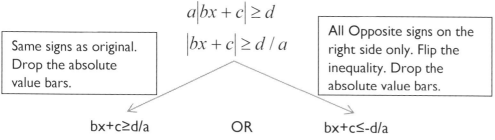

$$a\left|bx + c\right| \geq d$$

$$\left|bx + c\right| \geq d/a$$

Same signs as original. Drop the absolute value bars.

All Opposite signs on the right side only. Flip the inequality. Drop the absolute value bars.

bx+c≥d/a   OR   bx+c≤-d/a

- Solve for x from each.
  x≥(d/a −c)/b   OR   x≤(d/a+c)/-b (This changed to less than due to division by a negative number)

- Graph this range of values on the number line.
- Write in interval notation: Typical solution has two ranges of numbers going in opposite directions: (-∞, m]U[n, ∞)

Example: Solve $\frac{3}{5}$|2x-5|+6≥ 12

Solution: ISKSGI: Isolate, Separate, Keyword, Solve, Plot, Interval-Notation
First isolate the absolute value part

$$\frac{3}{5}|2x\text{-}5|\geq12\text{-}6$$

$$\frac{3}{5}|2x\text{-}5|\geq12\text{-}6$$

$$\frac{3}{5}|2x\text{-}5|\geq6$$

$$|2x\text{-}5|\geq6 \cdot \frac{5}{3}$$

$$|2x\text{-}5|\geq10$$

Separate, write keyword in between
2x-5≥10   OR   2x-5≤-10
Solve both new equations
2x≥15 OR   2x≤-5
x≥7.5   OR   x≤-2.5

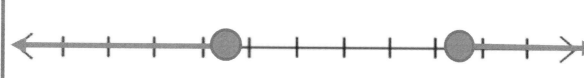

-2.5   **7.5**

- Interval Notation: (-∞, 2.5m]U[7.5, ∞)

268.   How do you graph an absolute value function in two variables?

Step 1) Graph the vertex

Step 2) Use the slope to find the second point, Join the line.

Step3) Draw the mirror image of points on the other side of the vertex. Join the line.

Example: $y=|2x+12|-4$

$y=2|x+6|-4$

Slope=2; Vertex: (-6,-4)

Picture53: Absolute Value Equation Graph of y=2|x+6|-4

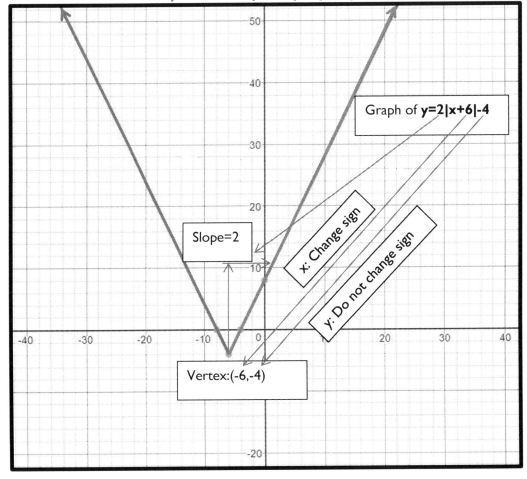

269.   **How do you graph an absolute value inequality function in two variables y≥a|x-h|+k?**

Step 1) Graph the vertex (h,k)

Step 2) Use the slope to find the second point

Step3) Draw the mirror image

Step4) Shade above or below depending on the inequality using a test point to check

Example: y≥|2x-4|+8

y≥2|x-2|+8

Vertex: (2,8) Slope=2

Picture54: Absolute Value Inequality Graph

(V shaped Shaded graph. Two lines due to absolute value sign, shaded due to inequality. "V" Facing up since slope is positive.)

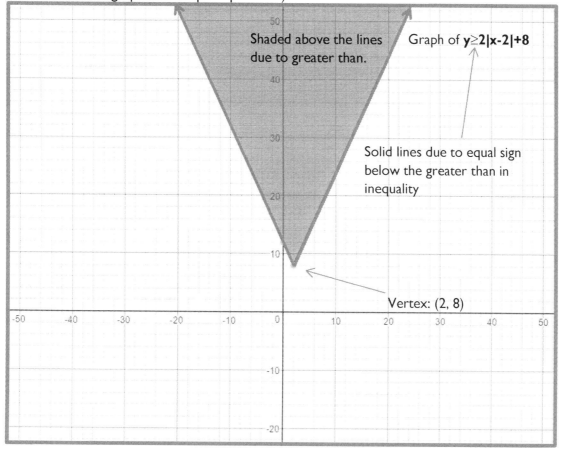

Shaded above the lines due to greater than.

Graph of **y≥2|x-2|+8**

Solid lines due to equal sign below the greater than in inequality

Vertex: (2, 8)

Vaishali Sudhakar has a Masters Degree in Chemical Engineering from the University of Houston. Her undergraduate education in Chemical Technology is from the Osmania University College of Technology, Hyderabad, India. She has been teaching math for over 15 years and has taught several math courses at colleges in the Houston Area. She has also worked as a private math tutor for several students. This course and the book are a result of her years of experience tutoring students. She firmly believes that an organized step-by-step methodology to learning Algebra I will be very valuable for both middle and high school students. "Many students think Math is difficult and that's because they have the fear of missing some information. Uncertainty in math creates fear. Organization of all the information is one important tool in learning math. Giving students all the concepts listed in one place in an orderly manner gives them a comprehensive guide to study at their own pace, and build their confidence of knowing all the rules. The best way to learn math is practice math. Writing concepts in a book and working many practice problems is the only way to master math. This book lists all the topics in an order such that there is no uncertainty. Let's simplify the learning process. There are different methods by which students learn but the common bottom line is to give them the confidence and tools to believe that they can achieve it." Vaishali's advice to teachers "First make the students comfortable listing the goals of the lesson so they know what to expect. Secondly use many different pictures, charts, and shapes in explaining concepts. Most students remember when a problem solution looks different from the others. Dedicate part of the class period for practicing what they have learnt in that class. Involve the students in explaining what they have learnt. Everyone is better prepared when they have to explain to others."

Student Testimonials

Mrs. Sudhakar's teaching methods prove to be very useful in the classroom as well as outside of class when assisting others and working on homework. She seeks to find easy methods for working problems and has mnemonics and other helpful strategies that allow the students to remember when to use a specific formula. Her teaching methods have proven to be successful as I started Algebra I with her as an 8th grade student with a B and continued on until Pre-Calculus where I received all A's. She instills the strategy in the students' brain by going over various practice problems that continually reinforce the topic. I am never afraid to ask her questions during my tutoring session as she is very considerate and compassionate towards her students. Overall, Mrs. Sudhakar's teaching methods have helped me overcome the toughest, in my opinion, high school math courses and have additionally enhanced my work ethic in not only math classes, but in all other classes as well.

A.M.(KatyISD)

Mrs. Sudhakar is an amazing, dedicated teacher who will go beyond what is necessary in order to ensure every student succeeds. I had trouble grasping a lot of the concepts in my higher level math classes, and she found various ways to help me understand and apply the skills. She would send me extra practice, helpful homework tips and prepare me for every test and quiz. She cares very deeply for every student she teaches and understands that every child learns differently, making her one of the best teachers I've had.

A.A.(KatyISD)

She's one of the most excellent tutors that I've ever had. Her system of teaching is so effective that I think I wouldn't have been able to get all A's in math without it. What she does when you come there to learn is first basically understand where you are and what you need help with in your math course. Then, she gives you practice problems and takes you step by step in problems which you don't understand. Then after you understand everything, she gives you practice for home to solidify everything that she explained to you. It's very effective!

H.K.(KatyISD)

Vaishali Sudhakar, my algebra tutor, is very mindful of her students and their personal learning styles. During my time under her tutoring I found myself comprehending things much quicker due to her various practice sheets that were adapted to every individual's style. As I was a visual learner she gave me many graphs, and visual aids to help the learning process. I enjoyed learning with her because she had many methods of learning and also allowed me to learn beyond my level, thus allowing growth within my math knowledge.

A.C.(KatyISD)

I like Mrs. Sudhakar's teaching because it's very personalized as to the style of explanation(learning through examples, or theorems, or re explanation) depending on the concept at hand and the level of confusion, this is always sure to provide a greater level of understanding. Secondly, she is always able to provide practice for my exact weaknesses instead of providing just general homework or not homework at all. Finally, she is able to provide a long-term solution to all errors that I make over and over again which improves my grades dramatically.

S.K(KatyISD)

72169750R00086